Jen —
Here's to your
Business Success!
Ride Hard!
Rich Allen
12/11

"Rich Allen's *Tour de Profit* provides a simple, yet powerful, roadmap to growth, profitability, and success in business and in life. His practical stage-by-stage approach provides owners and leaders of businesses of any size with a practical plan to win."

—**Sam Gilliland**, Chairman & CEO, Sabre Holdings

"This book provides a backbone of insightful business best practices organized around the metaphor of the bicycle. Rich's creativity, energy, and leadership abound in this well organized guide of how to improve your business. It is a practical "hands-on" book providing any business owner a challenge. The burden of leadership has to ask, "Are you up for the challenge?"

—**Pat Meyer**, President & CEO, Pella Corporation

"*Tour de Profit* will give you a clear path to success in your business. My experience with Rich Allen is he knows what it takes to win, and he's focused to a proven process to ensure results. Take advantage of his experience and knowledge and enjoy your ride to profitability."

—**Bill Darling**, President, Darling Homes

"*Tour de Profit* is a no nonsense practical guide for organizations looking for incremental and sustainable improvement in business and life. Rich Allen provides a solid roadmap when coupled with effective leadership will allow your team and business to reach heights you could have never imagined. "

—**Jay Arntzen**, President, Genesis Elevator Company, Inc.

"Rich has captured the tenacity of a cyclist in pursuit of business success. The "7 Keys to a Winning Team" combined with the other templates for improvement should equip the business to win in the marketplace."

—**Tom Commes**, Retired President, COO,
The Sherwin Williams Company

"This is not a quick-fix book. In today's world of one minute secretes to success Rich has the audacity to lay out a plan for learning how to win. He hits the fundamentals in clear and direct language and coaches the reader through the steps leading to lasting success. Rich knows what he is talking about both from personal experience in world-class companies and years of helping others. If you are serious about the goal and ready for the journey, I can think of no better guide."
  —Gary Christiansen, Retired CEO, Pella Corporation

"As a busy CEO in a rapidly growing company, this book was the perfect tool to allow me to re-evaluate our business. The 52 week, easy to read format worked perfect, and allowed me to set individual goals and milestones. The relation of business operations to a bicycle gave me an association that was both fun and helped in relating the materials making them easier to remember. I would definitely recommend taking the time to read this great business tool!"
  —Brian Dick, Chief Executive Officer,
  Quest Recycling Services

TOUR de PROFIT

A 52 Stage Race to Grow Your Business

by
Rich Allen

A.D. Ventures

Tour de Profit: A 52 Stage Race to Grow Your Business

Cover art by Azure Marketing
            www.azuremarcom.com
Editing and layout by Circumference Communication
            www.CircumferenceCommunication.com

ISBN: 978-0-9834926-2-7

Printed in the United States of America

"For I know the plans I have for you,"
declares the Lord,
"plans to prosper you
and not to harm you,
plans to give you hope
and a future."
– Jeremiah 29:11

To my loving wife, Drew,
who is my one-of-a-kind,

and my children,
Megan, Rhett and Anne Drew
for whom I race hard
everyday.

Table of Contents

FOREWORD

There are some things in life that appear to be complicated, such as being a parent, learning how to invest, and running your own business. But when we look more closely, you find that nothing could be further from the truth. Parents are taught by their children. Investors are taught by experience. And business owners should be taught by a mentor.

Going at it alone in business is difficult. At some point, it is easier to give up and quit trying.

The good news is there is help, and this book is the helping hand business owners need. My friend, Rich Allen, helps business owners take processes that appear to be complicated and make them achievable, if not extraordinarily simple.

You are holding in your hands a well-written, step-by-step guide through the basics and into a full blown race to business success.

When we learned to ride a bike as children, we fell down, scrapped our knees, maybe even scratched our bike. But with the encouragement and support of our parents and friends, we got back up, and tried again and again until we got it right.

Rich uses the bike as a metaphor for a business, and the Tour de France as a metaphor for the race toward success. Each week along the Tour de Profit, you will learn the fundamental concepts and techniques that we use at ActionCOACH to guide our business-owner clients through difficult challenges and decisions.

Many business owners over-complicate their role. They get distracted or derailed from their primary goals. In fact, many launch their business without a plan for winning. Most don't even know what it looks like to win.

The business coach's role is to help business owners map out their route to success. We help them assemble the knowledge and skills they need to complete the race. And we guide them along the course. Our proven models and methods have helped thousands of business owners around the world.

Rich has been an outstanding member of the Action-COACH team. His coaching experience, coupled with his previous experience growing sizable businesses, make him a valuable mentor to many business owners. In these pages, you will hear his passion for cycling, and understand why he applies the discipline of a long race like the Tour de France to business growth.

I encourage you to read this book with a purpose. The book is *not* designed to be read in one sitting. Instead, it will act as your guide for a solid year in the life of your business. Take the time to do the homework in each chapter. This is a long race, not a sprint; pace yourself.

I assure you, if you follow these simply, practical guides, you will learn how to be a better business owner, build a better team, and grow a stronger business.

Best of luck to you as you begin your Tour de Profit. I look forward to hearing your success stories.

Brad Sugars, Founder, Chairman, and President
ActionCOACH, the World's Number 1 Business Coaching Firm

Introduction

"What's best is when you're going faster than anybody else but you're not killing yourself, not subtracting from what you can do the next day."

- Lance Armstrong

What is the most grueling test of endurance in sports today? Many would suggest it is the Ironman Triathlon, which is three different sports (swimming, biking, and running) packaged together to create an almost impossible test of endurance.

Others might say it is the Western States 100, a 100-mile foot race over some of the most rugged terrain in the western part of the United States.

Or could it be the Tour de France, a 21-stage bike race that covers over 2,200 miles of some of the most challenging roadways in Europe?

It is hard to say which event is the most grueling. Without a doubt, they all demand a commitment and preparation.

In my opinion, the multi-stage bike race that is the Tour de France is the most challenging. No other sport requires the combination of preparation, training, mental toughness, teamwork, and flexibility as the Tour de France.

But when I extend my thinking beyond sport, the most grueling and challenging test of endurance that ordinary individuals face is easily owning, managing, and growing a business.

The challenges faced by business owners today rival any that can be found in the world of sport. And, unlike a sport, in business there is rarely substantial down time. While most sports have a "season," most businesses are ongoing—day after day, week after week—with no time to rest, recover, and recharge.

It is because of this that I have titled this book the *Tour de Profit: A 52 Stage Race to Grow Your Business*. Business is a weekly endurance test that stretches and strains the strongest professional. It is like a multi-stage bike race, except that the race extends throughout the year, and years to come.

Most business owners get trapped in the day-to-day grind of their business, and rarely spend time working on the things that matter most to build a solid, sustainable business.

Rather than measuring progress in a business on a monthly basis, it can be far more effective, and far more impactful, to think about each week as an opportunity to make a single improvement in your business. By working through 52 individual stages (weeks) throughout the year, you will accomplish more and grow your business faster.

Most progress occurs when there is incremental change that is accompanied with regular accountability. By focusing on weekly activities, tracking regular progress, and breaking down the large, strategic activities into bite-sized chunks, you can be more effective and more efficient in making positive change in your business.

How to Read this Book

This book is designed to give you a week-by-week guide of the critical stages of your business. Think of it as an instruction book to consistent and sustainable growth throughout the year.

The "chapters" or stages of this book are arranged in such a way as to give you a way to structure your time and efforts while working on business strategy and long-term growth.

While you may choose to read the whole book in a couple of sittings, or focus on a section at a time, I recommend returning to the pages at the beginning of each week to give you a focus for that week.

A quick and general overview will give you an idea of the course ahead and a sense of the individual stages, but each week you'll want to focus on a single stage. Make sure you not only master that stage that week, but that you also excel, even win, that stage.

THE EQUIPMENT

The bicycle is an excellent metaphor for a business. Many of the features and components of a bike can be viewed as powerful symbols for unique aspects of business. Let's take a quick lap around the bike from the perspective of a business owner.

Just as a bike has **handlebars** for steering, every business must be guided by the owner to where they want the business to go. The direction, adjustments, and ultimate destination are determined by how you move the handlebars. In business, the ultimate destination is determined by the vision, long-term goals, and near-term decisions you have. You decide where to steer your business.

Just as every bike has a **frame** that is best suited for the type of road that will be traveled on, every business has an optimum frame or structure to support the vision and long-term goals of the business.

The frame of a mountain bike is very different than a frame used for a road race. The frame of a bike sprinting in a velodrome is different from one used to tour a beach. As a business owner, you must make sure the frame of your business best matches the goals and terrain it will encounter.

In business, there are structures that may be appropriate for one business, but not for another. Many decisions must be considered to determine the best frame for a given business, but clearly there are some that are better than others for your business. Getting the frame/structure right is critically important.

The **front wheel** of the bike is like the sales and marketing aspects of the business.

The **spokes** are what give the front wheel its strength and ability to survive unexpected bumps in the road. If the front wheel were to have only two or three spokes, the wheel would not be particularly durable. A single pothole or pebble would cause the wheel to bend and break, which would bring the whole bike crashing down.

Therefore, the front wheel spokes represent your marketing strategies—the unique ways that potential customers come to know your business exists. In order for the business to be stable and durable, there must be six to eight, or even as many as ten, unique marketing strategies. With only two or three marketing strategies (spokes), the business is vulnerable to an inconsistent flow of new prospects—which could easily bring the business to a smashing halt.

Staying with the front wheel, the tire **tread** provides the traction that is needed to maintain a good grip on the road. The tread allows the rider to take corners at speed and make critical minor adjustments in direction. Often these slight adjustments lead to a win in a race.

Similarly, the front tire tread represents the unique sales process that you use to move prospective customers from simply knowing your business exists, to doing business with you.

The tread on the front tire of the business is critically important to sales success. Businesses without a specific, repeatable sales process tend not to be consistently capable of landing new customers. Their sales process is like a tire with bad tread, or inappropriate tread for the terrain.

The bike rider depends upon the **back wheel** of the bike for stability, grip, and traction. Most of the pressure on the bike gets transferred to the back wheel as the rider maneuvers through the racecourse.

Likewise, the back end of the business is where the pressure is greatest. Think of the back tire of your business as the process of delivering on the promises that were made to customers. The production processes must be dependable, reliable, repeatable, and sustainable. Any disruption in production or order fulfillment can cause stress within the business and has the potential to bring a business to an end.

The **gears and derailleur** give the rider the ability to race downhill at unbelievable speeds, and then power through serious mountain ascents. The ability to maintain a rhythm and cadence whether going uphill, downhill, or on a flat straightaway is important.

The gearing system and derailleur in a business are the continuous improvement processes and flexible processes that the business owner employs. Many businesses are seasonal, and must be able to adjust their operations efficiently to support their seasonal demands. As a business grows, it must be able to handle an ever-expanding customer base, while maintaining high quality standards and meeting customer delivery expectations. Gears are important to a business, just as they are to a bike.

Most bikes have a reliable **braking system**. There are times during a bike race where brakes must be applied to maintain control and gain stability.

In business, there must be financial controls that serve the same purpose. From time to time, every business must apply the financial controls on either the front wheel or the back wheel to maintain stability and control.

On the bike, the brakes must be directly wired so that when pressure is applied, the result is immediate and predictable. In your business, the financial controls must be directly wired so that when decisions are made, the results are predictable.

Bike riders track their progress by looking at their **indicators**. They often wear heart-rate monitors and have other gauges that indicate their pace and cadence. They know precisely how far they have traveled and their rate of speed. Without these indicators, it is difficult to make the necessary adjustments to win the race.

Businesses require similar indicators. There must be metrics on key performance indicators that help the business owner know what adjustments should be made. Without these indicators, the business owner is only guessing about what changes should be made. They must have data and intelligence on which to make decisions. Performance indicators provide the necessary intelligence to both the bike rider and the business owner.

On long rides, it is important to refresh and refuel. This is why many bikes are designed to carry **water bottles**. Being able to carry water or other nutrition is critical to keep the rider well hydrated and maintain their physical fitness level throughout the race.

Business owners require similar opportunities to refresh and refuel. From time to time, the business owner must step away from their business to spend time with their family, or to get away to think and perform longer term planning. Running a business is a marathon, not a sprint. During races, the business owner must find ways to get refreshed and refueled.

Every bike has a **seat**. This seat must be positioned exactly for the individual rider. The position, height, and design of the seat matters. Position accommodates the rider's height, weight, and pedaling style. The seat is set so the rider can transfer the maximum amount of power into the crank through their pedals.

In business, the seat represents the platform that supports the team. The business owner must have a support system, which allows team members to transfer maximum power into the work they do. The compensation system must be motivating, the benefits plan must provide peace of mind, the communications plan must deliver clear messages, and the rewards system must incent the desired behaviors. If these are all in place and well positioned, the people within the business will turn the crank and power the business faster and more efficiently than the competition.

So there you have it. The bike is a metaphor for a business. But that is not all. There are many other similarities between competing in a multi-stage bike race and successfully growing a business. We'll cover these in detail as we work through the book. But for now, I hope you get a sense of the power of the comparison.

My goal is to work with you through your own ride, and to show you how you can be more than competitive in your 52-stage race to grow your business. After all, your goal is to WIN!

Let's get started!

STAGE 1
Getting Started

Welcome to the Tour de Profit! You are about to begin a journey that will truly change the way you think about your business. Over the next 52 weeks, you will be introduced to proven, tested strategies and concepts that can transform your business from a so-so company into a best-in-class business.

Keep in mind, 52 weeks is a long time for any business leader to stay focused on a particular growth strategy. But if you are willing to put in the effort and follow this week-by-week guide, you will be rewarded with positive change the likes you have never seen before.

Since you are reading this book, I assume you are "in it to win it," and are ready to put forth the effort and consistency necessary to achieve success.

We've just started, and as they say in sports, "It's time to get your legs under you." No one starts the race with a sprint. The race we are on will take the whole year, so pace yourself. That's why we begin by setting a rhythm, finding your pace, and establishing consistent activities and behaviors.

So let's get on our bikes and get serious.

When we being a long race, it is important to start slowly. We know there are difficult stages ahead, but in this first stage, it is all about getting started, getting a feel for the race, setting the stage for what lies ahead, and generally getting used to the idea that we are in a race.

This book and the related website, tourdeprofit.com, are designed to guide you and help you win this important race. As we start, it is important that you take the time in this first stage to become familiar with the resources and support that you have around you.

You may want to look at a course map, so you can visualize where you will be racing. Visualization is important to anyone who likes competition. When you watch professional athletes in any sport, you will often see them close their eyes and visualize the shot, the play, the move.

As a business owner, you need to do the same thing. You need to visualize your desired outcome—get the picture clear in your head—and then you will be prepared when the moment comes to make your move and be successful.

The course map is posted on the tourdeprofit.com website. This will help you see where the race is going, the kind of terrain you will be covering, and what lies ahead for you.

While you are on the tourdeprofit.com website, take the time to check the other resources available to you. You will find many of the forms, worksheets, and documents mentioned in the different stages of the race under the "rider resources" tab. These are provided to enhance your ride, and give you a better chance at winning.

You will also note that there is a "riders only" section of the website. When you register as a rider, we will provide you with additional guidance, assistance, race updates, and race results. You can learn from others, and share your accomplishments with those also racing in the Tour de Profit.

Running a business can be lonely at times, the Riders Only section of the website allows you to connect with others who are focused on growing their businesses just as you are. So join in.

This is also the time to make a list of the big things you want to see changed in your business, or improved upon. By making the list now, you will be preparing yourself to pay attention to, and to focus on, during the difficult stages in your Tour do Profit.

Take a few minutes right now to list the top five things you would like to see changed in your business. What are the most significant points of pain for you as a business owner? Be honest with yourself, and write them down. You will be able to come back and reference these from time to time. As you proceed through the race, you will strike them off your list.

Item 1: _____

_____

Item 2: _____

_____

Item 3: _____

_____

Item 4: _____

_____

Item 5: _____

_____

As we begin the ride, and start to feel the easy pace of Stage 1, take time to mentally check your pre-race prep list. These are things you should make sure are done, ready, and in place so that when the racing really starts, you are ready to go hard.

Your list should include these items:

- Set aside time each week to focus on your Tour de Profit. I recommend at least one hour per week.

- Let your team know you are competing in this race. Consider having them ride the race along with you.

- Visit and explore the tourdeprofit.com website. Make sure you are gaining all the advantages you can.

- Prepare yourself and your team for change. If you read this book, and do nothing, you will get nothing from the effort.

- Begin planning for the celebrations that will come as a result of your wins. Make sure you celebrate the small victories along the way.

I hope you are as excited about the Tour de Profit as I am. I am confident that if you take this race seriously, dedicate time and effort, and maintain your commitment to the race, you will be hugely rewarded.

Just remember, you have a support team ready to help you. As you compete in the Tour de Profit, if you find that a task or assignment is not clear, or you need help completing it, please go to the tourdeprofit.com website, and click on the "rider Assistance" tab. Ask your question, and we will quickly respond. This way, you can quickly get back into the race.

We're off and racing! I tip my hat to you for suiting up, and climbing aboard. I look forward to your race updates along the way, and to hearing about your wins.

STAGE 2
Setting Your Goals

Now we're off. It's time to set our goals.

You might ask, why is this not Stage 1? Good question!

Actually, your goals should have been set well before this race began, but I am inserting it here "just in case" you happened to forget to set specific, measurable goals for your race.

It's okay to admit it. Most business owners go through the entire year without a real clear picture of the goals they have for their business. They are going through the paces, week after week, without a clue whether they are ahead or behind.

I think the reason most business owners do this is because if they never commit to a specific goal, they can't be disappointed when they miss it. It keeps them from feeling worse about their lack of a real plan to succeed.

But we're going to run this race differently. We're going to set very specific goals. We're going to make sure everyone on the team knows our goals, and we're going to measure our progress towards our goals on a regular basis.

Are you with me?

If so, let's get going on Stage 2: Setting Your Goals!

START HERE: Write down your goals for this year's race in the following categories. What do you want to accomplish in each particular area of your business?

Customer Satisfaction: _____
_____
_____
_____

New Market Expansion: _____
_____
_____
_____

Operational Efficiency: _____
_____
_____
_____

Revenue Growth: _____
_____
_____
_____

Profitability: _____
_____
_____
_____

If you have other specific areas that are critical to your success, then write down a goal in those areas as well. Be specific: _____

_____

_____

_____

Now, if your goals are for where you want to be by the end of the Tour de Profit, I want you to go back and break them up into quarterly goals. Rather than staring at huge, seemingly unachievable goals, it will be more motivating, more achievable if you state goals in quarterly terms. Where do you want to be by the end of March? How about the end of June? How about the end of September?

Customer Satisfaction:

January: _____

March: _____

June: _____

September: _____

New Market Expansion:

January: _____

March: _____

June: _____

September: _____

Operational Efficiency

January: _____

March: _____

June: _____

September: _____

Revenue Growth:

January: _____

March: _____

June: _____

September: _____

Profitability:

January: _____

March: _____

June: _____

September: _____

Other:

January: _____

March: _____

June: _____

September: _____

Making the goals more timely and achievable will motivate you and your team to accomplish them. If yours is a manufacturing business, or is dependent on daily, repetitive processes, then you may want to state your goals on a monthly, or even weekly, basis.

Now that you have your goals written, determine how you are going to share those goals with your partners, your team, and the person who is going to hold you accountable to them—your business coach.

You must go public with your goals if you intend to achieve them. Shine a light on them. Don't hide them just in case you do not achieve them or you can be certain about the future!

Lastly, begin measuring your progress against your goals. This is critical. Having a goal is one thing, but having a measurement system, so you can see your progress on a regular basis, is the key to victory!

Keep it simple. Find a place to record your progress on a daily, weekly and monthly basis. Share the results. Celebrate the small wins. Make corrections and adjustments on a regular basis. These tactics will keep you and your team focused, and will give you the highest probability of success.

Stage 2 is a critical part of this year's race. Take the time to record your goals NOW. You can thank me when you are standing on the winner's podium at the end of the Tour de Profit!

STAGE 3
Building Your Race Team

*W*ith goals in hand, and a commitment to measure your progress week after week, you are off and spinning! Hopefully your first couple of weeks have been both productive and invigorating. Momentum is building, and you are feeling good about your race plan and preparation.

Now, take a good look around, and ask yourself, "Do I have a good team of advisors to assist me as the race goes on?"

Admit it, you can't win the race on your own. You've got to surround yourself with strong talent in several key areas of support. Certain people will be needed at different stages. Are they now in place?

Let's start with the basics. Do you have a stellar **CPA** on your team? You need more that a bookkeeper who will record your financial entries. You also want an accountant who knows your business, your plans, and your long-term goals? If you do not have this person, get them. Talk with other business owners, ask them for their recommendations, and then spend the time to meet, interview, and select the right CPA for you.

How about your **business attorney**? Do you have a close relationship with a legal professional who can guide you through the challenging decisions during this race? You must have someone who is solid technically, determined to defend your position, and caring enough to understand your "why."

Ask yourself, "Who will hold me accountable for my personal actions and behaviors?" Probably not your spouse. Probably not your business partner. Probably not your employees. If you want to achieve your big dreams, then you must have a **business coach**, someone who will help you think through your most challenging business issues, and hold you accountable.

There are several other professionals you need on your team: a **business banker**; a **commercial insurance agent**; a **human resources professional**; and a **financial planner,** for both your personal finances and for your team (401k's, savings plans, retirement accounts, etc.). If you have heavy administrative work, then hire support, or better yet, get a virtual assistant.

Don't make the mistake that many business owners do. They think they are super human and can handle all of the details themselves. Many can, but when they do, they take their focus off of the marketplace and off of the customers. It's hard to tell how many opportunities are lost or squandered because the business owner was focused on handling payroll or other activities that should have been done by someone for $15 per hour. Don't let this happen to you!

If you want this to be your best year ever, take the time to build a strong team around you. Stay focused on the strategy, the sales, the customers, and how well you are delivering on your promises. Leave other activities to those who are better suited, and more skilled, to handle them.

Make sure you fill in each of the below fields this week. If this stage does not get done this week, focus on this stage until each position is filled. Remember, you can't finish the next stage until you've finished this one.

CPA: _____

Attorney: _____

Business Coach: _____

Business Banker: _____

Insurance Agent: _____

HR Professional: _____

Financial Planner: _____

Once these key positions are in place, you are ready to face future stages. You need a support team to complete the race. If any of these people is missing, you will find yourself in dire situations during the course. It's better to have the people in place now than to scrounge for them in the moment of crisis.

After all, your goal is to win the race, not to sprint through a few stages and give up. Prepare for success. Instead of fixing your own bike, replenishing your water, and doing your own repairs, have the people in place who will help you complete the race successfully. Stage 3 is critical to freeing you up to lead your company.

STAGE 4
Your Value Proposition

*S*tage 4 is the most important stage of the race. You're off to a great start—you have your goals set, you are measuring your progress on a regular basis, and you have your support team in place. Celebrate!

You're still in the early stages of the race, and you have to maintain momentum while you deliver VALUE to your clients and customers. But ask yourself, "What exactly is my Value Proposition?" You must know it and be able to deliver it day in and day out—without exception.

So, what is your Value Proposition? Many business owners respond with something like, "excellent customer service," or "quality products and services." Others will suggest it has something to do with their reputation or their long history of excellent performance. I believe it must be stated in terms of a FEELING that someone gets when they do business with you.

That's right, a FEELING! Have you ever defined your Value Proposition in terms of a feeling? Think about it. When a customer uses your product or service, how does that make them FEEL? Do they get a sense of confidence? Do they feel refreshed? Does working with you give them a sense of hope? Maybe when they visit your shop they are overwhelmed by a sense of calm relaxation. What is it that you want them to FEEL?

Write it down right now:

Our customers feel _____ _____ when they do business with us.

This is not a "touchy-feely" activity. This is a critically important assessment of what you are trying to accomplish in your business. The feelings your customers get when they do business with you have everything to do with your reputation. Feelings generate emotion. Emotion drives commitment. You want your reputation in the marketplace to be firmly linked to the desired feelings your customers have when they do business with you.

Let's face it, most of us do not have name recognition like Coke or McDonalds. Most of us also do not have a product that is as well known as Apple or Kleenex. Most of our customers buy from us because of how they feel when they do business with us. That is what keeps them from going to your competitors.

Here is a simple exercise for you this week: Ask some of your current customers, what they feel when they do business with you. That's right, ask them why they buy from you and not from your competitors.

It is scary how many business owners don't take the time to ask their current customers why they do business with them. Maybe because they are afraid of the answer. Maybe they are worried their customer may say, "Gee, I don't really know why. Maybe I should try the other guy!"

Ask your customers! Ask several of them. When you get several who share a similar feeling with you, you will know exactly why they do business with you. Think about it, how can you ever replicate what matters to your customers if you don't know what matters to them? Your customers will tell you what your Value Proposition is—or should be!

So, Stage 4 is a difficult stage. You can't give an off-the-cuff response to your value proposition. It must be thoroughly researched. But, once you have it, you will be in a position to really pick up the pace as you head into the next stages of this critical race.

Work hard during this stage to determine exactly what your Value Proposition is. I guarantee it will help you as the Tour de Profit heats up in the coming weeks!

STAGE 5
Bring Your Value Proposition to Life

Your Tour de Profit is well underway!

So how is it going for you? Four stages are behind you—your first month into the year. By now you should be rolling along, creating raving fans, and landing new clients. How are you feeling? Winded? Tired? Fired Up? Encouraged?

We've covered some important territory during the first four stages:

- Tracking daily and weekly activity
- Writing goals for the year
- Sharing your goals with your team
- Assembling your team of advisors
- Refining your Value Proposition
- Visiting with many of your current customers to get their inputs on your Value Proposition

That's a lot of ground to have covered. Notice how much you can accomplish with a little work each week.

Now to Stage 5. It is time to bring your Value Proposition to life. You've spent the time thinking about it, and asking others, "Why do you do business with me?" Their answers are the clues to the "feelings" that your customers get when they do business with you. Now, it is time to bring this feeling to life in your business.

This week, I want you to ask what you need to do everyday to make sure you deliver your Value Proposition to your customers. If you are in the business of building self esteem, then how are you going to do that? What activities will you do? It may be using your customer's name when you greet them, or using uplifting words with your customers to make them feel important. Get specific. What will you do to deliver on the feeling you want your customers to have when they do business with you?

Make a list of these critical behaviors. My bet is that you will need to change your behavior, and many behaviors of your team, in order to deliver your true value proposition.

_____

_____

_____

_____

_____

_____

_____

It will be difficult to achieve your list. You will certainly stumble from time to time. But, if you truly work at it, I can guarantee that you and your business will push ahead of your competition, and your customers will reward you for your efforts!

So, make a commitment during this stage. Make the commitment that you will do the following:

- Translate your Value Proposition into a list of activities that you will do everyday when you are face to face with your customers or prospects.

- Communicate your list of activities to your team and hold them accountable to behave differently from this week forward.

- Recognize your team members when they perform the daily activities that you have listed. Rather than be critical, find the successes and reward them!

It's that simple—three action items for you at this stage. Set aside the time to get this done. This is truly where the "rubber meets the road." Anyone can come up with a clever Value Proposition statement. Only few will do the work necessary to bring it to life.

If you intend to win the Tour de Profit, you MUST complete these three action items this week.

STAGE 6
Start
Stop
Improve

Stage 6 of the Tour de Profit is the last stage related to your Value Proposition.

If you've been doing your work, you now have your Value Proposition well defined. Your current customers have helped you think about the value you deliver, in terms of the "feelings" they get when they do business with you. You've taken their advice and lined up your internal processes to deliver those "feelings" every time you interact with a client or prospect.

Good for you! Your efforts in these first five stages of the race are setting you up to shift gears, move faster, and exert less energy as the 52-stage race continues.

But, before we leave the Value Proposition subject, there is one last piece of work for you to do. You need to answer three very important questions:

What must I START DOING to deliver my Value Proposition? Limit the things you should start doing to a critical few items. Never attempt to totally overhaul your processes. Simply identify the two or three things that are most important in the delivery of your Value Proposition and add them to your processes. These should be high impact additions. If something does not have high impact, leave it for another time. _____

_____

_____

What must I STOP ALLOWING to deliver my Value Proposition? This is the most critical question of the three. In order to give yourself more freedom and flexibility to make changes, you need to identify those activities that are simply wasting your time and not adding to your value. If you give this some thought, you will absolutely identify activities that you can stop, and replace them with those you must START DOING. Don't brush this question aside. Focus on it hard. There is gold in this question! _____

_____

_____

What must I IMPROVE? What am I currently doing that needs to be better? There are things you are doing correctly today, but maybe just not consistently or in the most professional way. Identify these and take the time to make them better. Give them more of a priority and a commitment. Package these improvements with those activities you will START DOING, and make sure they are not crowded out by those activities you are going to STOP

DOING; these will be game-changing improvements for your business. _____

_____

_____

These are critical questions you must focus on, and answer, in order to make your business better.

Many business owners come across new ideas and simply add them to the many things that were once priorities in their business. They never take the time to ask these three questions. If they would, their efforts would return the benefits they desire.

So, there it is. Stage 6 is as easy as focusing on three critical questions, and taking the time to make the changes you identify permanent and consistent.

You may need to reinforce these new behaviors within your team. They will naturally resist changes, but if you are committed to this race, then you will NOT ALLOW anyone to knock you off course!

Three simple questions...massive improvements in the value you deliver to your customers! Take the time to focus during this stage.

STAGE 7
Time Trial #1:
Your Non-negotiables

It is hard to believe it, but we are already in the 7th Stage of the Tour de Profit! How are you feeling? Are you getting enough sleep? Are you eating well?

How is your team doing? Are they motivated and working hard for you?

Succeeding at business is no easy task. It takes 100% effort from everyone on the team. Everyone must be pulling in the same direction. You must be providing the kind of inspirational leadership that causes people to go the extra mile—not because they have to, but because they want to!

I heard Keith Cunningham, author of *Keys to the Vault*, say that the power in any organization comes from only two places:

1. The people you hire and train
2. The culture you create in your business

I completely agree with this statement. The people you hire, the training you give them, and the expectations you set for behaviors and performance, are what set your business apart from every other business out there.

I would go a step further to say that the culture you create is the number one most important factor in defining the kind of business you will have. So, with that being the case, what is the culture in your business?

Would I be able to see it, feel it, sense it, if I were to meet you or one of your team members?

Would it jump out at me if I walked into your place of business?

Is it real or are you just "wishing" it was a particular way?

Stage 7 is your first time trial of the tour. This week's task is relatively simple, but it is often overlooked by business owners. Your challenge is to get down on paper the six to eight specific things that you consider to be non-negotiable in your business. Sounds easy doesn't it? Then do it right now!

Ask yourself these questions:

What would I simply not tolerate from one of my team members? _____

_____

How do I expect my customers to be treated? _____

_____

_____

What impression do I want to give everyone who comes in contact with our company? _____

_____

_____

What would really set me off and push me over the edge? _____

_____

What would make me walk someone to the door without a second thought? _____

_____

_____

What else will I not allow? _____

_____

_____

I know some of these questions are stated in the negative, but, if you can capture the passion and energy that often comes from frustration, then you can later re-word your statements to be in the positive.

Your time trial is about to start? You have only **ten minutes** to complete this assignment.

In ten minutes list the first six to eight non-negotiables that come to mind. Don't wordsmith them. Write them as you think and feel them. Use your words, not corporate speak.

Ready? GO!

Number 1: _____

Number 2: _____

Number 3: _____

Number 4: _____

Number 5: _____

Number 6: _____

Number 7: _____

Number 8: _____

Now that you have your list, refine them this week into a nice, tight, descriptive set of values for your business. We will call this list your Culture Statement.

Not sure if you have them right? Ask a friend or associate. If you speak directly and clearly, they will recognize the words as being yours.

Winning this stage will re-energize your business!

STAGE 8
Assessing Your Competition

So, how did you do in your time trial last week? Were you able to come to a clear definition of your non-negotiables? Did you take the time to share them with your business partners? How about with your team? Do you have them written down? Excellent!

If you did your work well, you will refer to your list of non-negotiables often, and they will guide you through some very difficult situations and tough decisions.
Now do what most business owners fail to do—LIVE BY THEM! If your non-negotiables become just words on a page, you'll be like millions of other business owners who talk the talk, but won't walk the walk.

Now on to Stage 8. Hard to believe we are already eight stages into the Tour de Profit! Looking back, you've covered a lot of ground, and hopefully you have put yourself in a nice position at the end of your second month of this race.

As we head into the difficult stages that lie ahead, we must get a good assessment of our competition. We must know where we have advantages and where we have weaknesses. We must prepare ourselves to take advantage of opportunities, and plan for and prepare to survive the threats that our competitors are sure to launch at us.

Look at your competition. Do you notice anything different about their strategies this year? Have they bulked up for this race, or have they slimmed down to be in better shape? Is their team better than last year? Are they riding new equipment?

How well do you know your competition? How much time do you spend gathering information about them? Are you silently observing them, sizing them up, comparing their approach to yours? Be on your toes, and gather critical data to help you be more successful.

You may be familiar with the term SWOT Analysis. SWOT stands for **Strengths**, **Weaknesses**, **Opportunities,** and **Threats**. It is a well-documented methodology for analyzing your competition. If you want to win the Tour de Profit, you can't do it without knowing whom your racing against. You must know where you stand RELATIVE to your competition. The SWOT Analysis will help put your business into perspective.

Doing a SWOT Analysis is very simple. Make a list of all your Strengths, Weaknesses, Opportunities, and Threats on the following pages:

My Strengths: _____

_____
_____
_____
_____
_____
_____
_____
_____
_____
_____
_____
_____
_____
_____

My Weaknesses: _____

_____
_____
_____
_____
_____
_____
_____
_____
_____
_____
_____
_____
_____
_____

My Opportunities: _____

_____
_____
_____
_____
_____
_____
_____
_____
_____
_____
_____
_____
_____
_____
_____

My Threats: _____

_____
_____
_____
_____
_____
_____
_____
_____
_____
_____
_____
_____
_____
_____
_____

Over this next week, as you think about, observe, and gather information about your main competitors, add to what you've written here. Be candid with yourself. This exercise is not being scored or evaluated. You are going to use it to give yourself the advantage. But first you must collect the data and fill in the pages.

Once you have your four sections filled with notes, the magic happens.

Take your Strengths list and your Opportunities list, and ask yourself, "What could I do, using my strengths, to take advantage of my opportunities?"

Make a new list of the things you could do to "leverage" your strengths to take advantage of your opportunities.

Next, take your Weaknesses list and your Threats list, put them side by side, and ask yourself, "What must I do right now to shore up my weaknesses and eliminate the possible threats?" There may be one or two critical things you must do now to cover your flank.

Most business owners fail to do this part of the exercise. They do a SWOT Analysis, but never do anything with it.

If you want to win the Tour de Profit, you must TAKE ACTION on your SWOT Analysis!

You have a big assignment for Stage 8. Carve out the time to get it done!

STAGE 9
Critical Skills Required for Success

L ast week was an important week in the Tour de Profit. You spent time doing a SWOT Analysis, examining your strengths and weaknesses relative to your competition.

Often, we think we have the advantage when we see our competitors' faults. It is harder to look introspectively and be honest and candid with ourselves about our short-comings and weaknesses. I hope you were truly honest with yourself, and identified those areas where you need to get better in your business.

Stage 9 focuses on doing something about the SWOT Analysis you completed last week. It does you no good to do the SWOT Analysis and simply put it on the shelf. You must now decide what you need to do with what you now know.

The key to turning your SWOT Analysis into a win for your business is to ask yourself, "What critical skills am

I lacking in my business?" These may be skills that you know you don't have or talents lacking in your team.

Often, I see business owners who are willing to "get by" with the skill set they have, even when they are lagging behind their competitors. Why? Because confronting the reality of the situation is hard!

It is hard to admit to yourself that you are not as good as you need to be in a particular skill or competency area. It is often harder to confront a long-time team member with the fact that they are not skilled enough to perform the tasks you now need done. Stepping up to the realities of your situation takes courage and commitment.

So, here is your assignment for this week: Identify the three or four critical skills or talents that you lack in your business. Be totally honest with yourself. If you are not particularly good at prospecting for new customers, then write it down. If you don't have a handle on your financials, then write it down. Whatever you are lacking, write them below.

In order to beat my competition, I must improve my ability to

1) _____

2) _____

3) _____

4) _____

Next, look over your SWOT Analysis and determine the areas where you need to FOCUS your improvement efforts. The first step towards improvement comes from identifying the issues in specific terms.

Now, under each of the three or four Critical Skills or Talents you lack, write down what you are going to do to resolve the issues. It may require specific training. It may require bringing in someone who can help you get better. It may mean moving someone from one role to another, or even having to ask someone to leave the business. Don't let your fear of the change stop you from dealing with the issue!

I am going to resolve issue (   ) by _____

_____

_____

_____

I am going to resolve issue (   ) by _____

_____

_____

_____

I am going to resolve issue (   ) by _____

_____

_____

_____

I am going to resolve issue (   ) by _____

_____

_____

_____

Do you have your list together? Are your three to four weaknesses identified clearly? Are your action items specific? Could an outsider look at your list and know exactly what to do, and when? Make sure every action item is Specific, Personal, Actionable and Measureable. I like to call this "SPAMing" your goals!

This week, turn your SWOT into SPAM (Specific, Personal, Actionable, Measureable) goals to shore up the areas of your business where you lack critical skills and talents. Do this, and you will gain ground on your competition— and leave many of them wondering how you managed to put your business into another gear.

Action:
    Specific: _____
    Personal: _____
    Action: _____
    Measurable: _____

Action:
    Specific: _____
    Personal: _____
    Action: _____
    Measurable: _____

Action:
    Specific: _____
    Personal: _____
    Action: _____
    Measurable: _____

Action:
    Specific: _____

    Personal: _____

    Action: _____

    Measurable: _____

Make Stage 9 a game-changer for your business!

MASTERY REGION

STAGE 10
Financial Mastery

You've been in the race for 9 weeks now. You're fast approaching the one-quarter mark in the race. Yes, it is hard to believe that we are almost ¼ of the way through the race already! Hopefully, by now you have made some significant changes in your business that will position you to do well in the next critical stages of the Tour de Profit.

As we begin Stage 10, we enter the Mastery region of the Tour. You will be racing in the Mastery region for several weeks. These are critical, foundational weeks in the race where you focus on the fundamentals that will be necessary for the more difficult stages ahead. One of the fundamental concepts ActionCOACH uses is to help business owners establish Mastery in their business. Most business owners believe they have mastery of their business; let's not just "hope"; let's make certain that we do!

The first stage in the Mastery region is Financial Mastery. Financial mastery is one of the skills, capabilities, and toolsets you must have in your business to be successful.

This week, your assignment is to be certain that you have the fundamental financial insights in your business to help you make great decisions.

Ready? Let's get started!

Financial mastery begins with having access to your business financial reports on a regular and timely basis. You should be reviewing three critical financial reports on a monthly basis:

1. Profit & Loss Statement (P&L)

2. Balance Sheet

3. Cash Flow Statement

These three financial documents will tell the story of your business. Together, they paint a powerful picture of how well your business is performing, where your opportunities for improvement are hiding, and what the near -term outlook is from a financial perspective. It is critical that you have these prepared on a timely basis and review them monthly.

Are you?

Once you have your monthly financial reports available, you are in a position to track some key indicators of success. These are important ratios and measures that you can lift from your financial statements and track on a regular basis. You not only want to know where your business is at, but rather how your business is doing relative to the past months, perhaps even to the same month of prior years.

Have you identified your key indicators of success?

Key indicators of success are best viewed on a dashboard—a visible set of graphs that tell a story of the health and trends in your business. Your dashboard should be updated at least monthly. It should be much like the dashboard of a car, allowing you to look forward, rather than in the rear-view mirror.

Included in your Dashboard should be activities that are not found in your financial statements. They should reflect your lead generation and lead conversion success rates, as well as other delivery and customer satisfaction measures.

Is your Dashboard up and visible? Are you aware of the trends in your business?

Being successful in Financial Mastery involves your mindset. You must have the mindset to demand you have the financial data needed to run your business.

How can you know if you are winning if you do not know the score? You must be looking at your scorecard on a regular basis, and using your scorecard to help you make great decisions in your business.

As you gain mastery in this area, you will expect and demand even more. You can begin looking at the individual profit margins by product or service type. You can see labor rates and overhead percentages, and many more critical metrics.

There is a saying that speed kills. The faster you want to go in your business, the better set of financial indicators you must have. Going fast is good only if you have the financial awareness, and can read the Financial Dashboard.

During this stage of the race, take time to nail down your Financial Mastery. Expect and demand regular reports, graphs, matrixes, and indicators that will let you race even faster—without the fear of not knowing where you are headed, or whether you have enough energy and stamina!

Stage 10 is the first stage in the Mastery Region of the Tour de Profit. You must win this stage to position yourself for success in the stages that follow.

STAGE 11
Delivery Mastery

You're riding in the MASTERY region of the Tour de Profit. How has the ride been for you? Are you gaining confidence? Are you learning skills that will help you win the race? Are you staying on top of your game? Are you staying motivated and enthusiastic about the difficult stages that lie ahead? I sure hope so.

This week we enter Stage 11: Delivery Mastery. With ten stages behind us, it is time to be certain that we have the fundamentals of execution firmly in our business. Our customers are returning to buy from us not only because we have a great product, but also because they know HOW we deliver it—it's what sets us apart from our competition.

Think about it. You frequent a business not only because you like the product they offer, but also because of the service they deliver. How often do you return to a business when the service is below your expectation? Maybe you'd go one more time because you're a nice person, and want to give them the benefit of the doubt, but if the service they provide is sub-par on the second visit, you probably will go to their competition next time.

The same is true for your customers. Every time they walk into your store, visit your office, or talk with you on the phone, they are evaluating the service you are providing. If your interaction with them is below their expectations, they will begin thinking about how to get what they need from another source. You must be tuned in to how your customers are feeling about doing business with you. I call this Delivery Mastery.

You must "master" the art of delivering great service to your customers. You cannot rely on your team if they do not have, or do not know, your customer service standards. These standards must be specifically designed for your business, and include the processes, tools, and methods that define high standard of delivery.

To begin, you must know your goals for delivery. You must have a good idea of the "feeling" you want your customers to have when they do business with you. This will be the basis for the specific step-by-step processes that you will use to deliver that "feeling" each and every time you interact with your customers.

Write down the feeling you want your customers to have when they do business with you?_____

_____

_____

_____

Next, you must understand the critical elements of success for delivery performance. How critical is having the right inventory available for your customers? What impression do potential customers get when they look at your storefront or office? How critical is the quality of the product you are delivering? How about the tone of voice you, or your team, use when speaking with your customers?

Each of these impressions influences the delivery experience that your customers have. As the business owner, you must set the standards you expect in each of these areas of delivery.

Level of inventory you want to maintain: _____

_____

Cleanliness of your shop or office: _____

_____

Dress of your team members: _____

_____

On a separate sheet, create the scripts that will be used when answering the phone. Make sure each team member uses these scripts.

Now here comes the big assignment of the week: ask your current customers how they FEEL about doing business with you. Ask them specifically what "feelings" come to mind when they think about doing business with your company.

Business owners often avoid this task because they don't want to know the answers. It is critical that you know what they are feeling. If their feelings don't line up with your expectations, it is your responsibility to make the necessary changes.

Your challenge during Stage 11 is to not only define your expectations for delivery, but to also make sure your customers are experiencing those expectations. You also need to make sure your customers experience these every time they visit your business. Hold your team accountable to these delivery standards and you will be well on your way towards Delivery Mastery in your business!

STAGE 12
Time Mastery

Welcome to Stage 12 of the Tour de Profit!
You have just completed a very critical ride in Stage 11 where you worked on your Delivery Mastery. What changes did you make to your execution and delivery systems? Did you ask your current customers how satisfied they were with your current level of service? Did you get some great feedback? More important, did you use the feedback to make changes in what you do on a daily basis? If so, then it was a great stage win for you!

This week we continue our Tour de Profit in the Mastery Region. Your assignment this week is to tackle one of the most difficult challenges facing business owners today, how to efficiently utilize your most valuable resource—your TIME!

Time Mastery is a challenge for everyone in business. It is especially challenging for the senior-most person in any organization. This is one area where you must pay attention and learn how to improve.

How you spend your time in your business will have a significant influence on how successful you are as a business owner. Others will judge what is truly important to you by how you spend your time. I can assure you that if your team sees you spending time behind your computer, they will know that computer work is important to the business. If they see you spending time with your customers, they will know that customers are important to you and to the business. You set the tone for your team by how you spend your time.

You can categorize the use of time into one of four categories:

- Not Urgent and Not Important
- Urgent but Not Important
- Urgent and Important
- Not Urgent but Important

These may sound like strange definitions, so let me restate them in more familiar terms: Distractions, Delusions, Demands, and Strategies.

Things like e-mail and surfing the web are often **Not Urgent and Not Important**, or **Distractions**. You must avoid spending too much time on these activities during the day.

Many phone calls and walk-in requests fall into the category of **Urgent but Not Important**, or **Delusions**. People come to you because someone else did not do what they were supposed to, or because there is no process in place to handle the situation.

Many customer calls or production issues are **Urgent and Important**. They are **Demands** that must be handled to satisfy a customer, or keep the operation moving, but they suck time from you largely because there is no system in place to make sure the issue is handled the first time.

The biggest challenge for you as a business owner is to spend as much time as possible on those issues that are **Not Urgent but Important**. These are the **Strategic** decisions that will determine where you focus in your business. They are not urgent, so they often get pushed back in the priority stack where they can be forgotten. As the business owner, it is your job to focus your time on these areas of your business.

So how do you focus on the Not Urgent but Important? One practical idea is to block time on your calendar for critical tasks you must do, even though there is no emergency driving them. I call this process using a Default Calendar. When you put the big, critical items into your calendar first, you will always find time to fit in the other, smaller items.

List those items that are Not Urgent but Important for your business. By writing them down, you are making a commitment to place these items into your schedule:

_____

_____

_____

_____

_____

_____

_____

Don't just put these important items into your calendar; FOCUS ON THEM! Resist the urge to blow right past them or put them off. Discipline yourself to focus first on the strategic, operational, and execution-oriented activities.

How you spend your time will determine your ultimate level of success. You need to be doing the $200 per hour jobs while you are having someone else do the $10 per hour jobs. Don't get stuck spending your time doing things you could easily pay someone else to do.

Have a good ride this week! I'll be looking for you at the finish line of Stage 12: Time Mastery.

STAGE 13
Destination Mastery

Itrust you are entering Stage 13 with a new found sense of priorities. You are now effectively using your valuable time.

In Stage 12, we talked about how to focus your attention on those things that are Important but Not Urgent in your business, those things that will shape your future and motivate your team. If you missed the last stage, take the time to go back and do what is important, but not urgent, for your business.

In this week's stage, we are moving forward to a new area of Mastery: Destination Mastery. Yes, believe it or not, many business owners are running their business without a clear idea of where they intend to take the business. Often, we get so buried in the day-to-day that we forget why we went into business in the first place. Before you go one more week, take time to focus on your future. The clarity you get from doing this may change the "so what" for you and your business.

I can't tell you how many times I've asked a business owner, "What do you want this business to be in five years?" and they cannot answer with clarity. Even scarier is when the business owner cannot answer the question, "What is your ultimate exit plan for your business? Are you planning ultimately to sell, transition to your children, go public, or what?" Have you thought through these questions for your business?

What you ultimately intend to do with your business is critical to many legal and financial aspects of your business. Let's face it, every business goes through transitions. Your business will likely face death, divorce, sale, closure, IPO, employee buyout, transfer to family or friends, and so on during its life cycle. You can chose to plan for your preferred transition, or you can let it just happen to you. I would suggest that planning has far more benefits than taking a "whatever" attitude.

Let's focus on the positive aspects of the future. The first thing you need to have clearly in your mind is your growth goal. Are you thinking of expanding geographically? Will you be opening new offices? If so, where? Will you be expanding into new product areas? Are you planning to grow organically (internally) or through acquisitions? How aggressively are you planning to grow the business?

In the space below, write down your ultimate goal for your company: _____

_____

_____

_____

Not only do you need to be clear about the direction of your company, your team members also need to know your plans. Can you see how knowing your ultimate goals with conviction and clarity will motivate your team? Some may be scared by your big plans, but I can assure you, people like to work with those who have a vision and a dream. It generates excitement and gets people seeing themselves as a bigger part of a business that is going somewhere.

As the business owner, your primary role is to create a vision and picture for the future that is exciting, compelling, and motivating to others. Without a clear idea of your future destination, everything falls flat.

Once you get the picture clear in your head, then share it with your team—on a regular basis. Show them how you are making progress towards the Big Dream. Let them be a part of your dream. Let them see themselves as part of the success. Their productivity, commitment, and passion for your success will rise to heights you have never seen before.

Meanwhile, behind the scenes, dedicate some of your time this week to seek out wise counsel on how to best structure your business entity, your financials, and your ownership structure, for an orderly transition to your ultimate exit strategy.

Let me be clear. It is critical that you have the legal, financial, and ownership issues in place well before you plan to exit your business. It will lessen your stress level, reduce your expenses related to the transition, and make it a pleasant experience.

Take time this week to get your thinking straight on where you want to take your business—in the near term and over the long-term. The effort you put forth during this Stage 13 will pay you dividends for years to come!

Ride hard this week! You're doing great and positioning yourself to win the Tour de Profit!

STAGE 14
Quality Time with Your Family

You've worked hard for 13 straight weeks. You're off to a great start, but this is a long race. You need to pace yourself so that you can be fresh and sharp for the difficult race stages that lie ahead.

This week, Stage 14, is an off week—a rest week. It is time to get off the bike, take a break, and focus on the other important things in your life.

But before we do that, let's take a quick look back to the Mastery stages. We've covered four areas that are critical to the success of your business: Financial Mastery, Delivery Mastery, Time Mastery and Destination Mastery. I cannot emphasize enough how important it is to get these very specific elements nailed down in your business. Without them all you have is chaos! Master these four areas, and you will create the foundation on which you can build your winning business. If you missed one of these stages, then take the time right now to go back, review and get rock solid on them. You will thank yourself later.

Stage 14 is about taking time to spend with your family or significant non-work friends. For some of you, this will be a difficult week. You may find it hard to believe that your business can indeed function without you, but you will have to trust me that it can and will.

Your assignment this week is to leave your desk behind, put your laptop in its case, turn off your cell phone, and focus your attention on spending quality time with those who love you.

Quality time is defined as time where there are no external distractions, where you are fully present in the moment and not thinking or worrying about business.

Can you accomplish this? This is your week to prove your skills in this area.

You may need to arrange for a few administrative changes. There may be signature authority that needs to be given. You may have to publish "acting" responsibilities, so that your team members know who to look to for guidance and assistance while you're out. You may even need to pre-pay some expenses or coordinate bank deposits. No matter what, you need to find a way to delegate responsibilities to others, so that you can take time off without having to be in the office physically and emotionally.

Now that you have made the necessary arrangements, the more important assignment for the week is to determine what you are going to do to spend quality time with your most special people. There is no need to travel, to add complexity to the week, or to schedule every minute of every day. Just decide how you are going to spend your week.

And whatever you do, do it with gusto! Play like you mean it. Let those around you know you have as much energy and excitement about them as you do your business. Do not short-change yourself this week. Make it special! Make it matter! Make it one to remember!

NICHE
REGION

STAGE 15
Creating a Unique Selling Proposition

It is hard to believe that we are already into Stage 15 of this year's Tour de Profit! We've successfully navigated our way through the Mastery Region, and are now ready to take on another significant challenge—the Niche Region.

But, as they say, the race continues! Stage 15 takes us into a new region: the Niche Region. This is where we answer the critical questions, and put in place the essential elements to make sure we can make a profit in our business. It has often been said that without a niche, the only option is to compete on price! Unless you are as efficient as Wal-Mart or FedEx, you don't stand a chance at competing only on price.

So how can you move away from competing on price? Many business owners swear that their industry has "deteriorated" to price competition only. I totally disagree with that assessment in any industry. Ask yourself, why do people pay $3 or $4 or more for a cup of coffee at Starbuck's, when they can get a larger one from a convenience store for $1.95? Why would you ever buy a bagel with cream cheese for $4 at Panera's, when you can buy them by the dozen for about the same price at a grocery store? Why do people shop at Nordstrom's, when they can find similar styles and fashions at Target? Understanding the WHY is the key to answering these questions.

Each of the businesses I just mentioned have spent time determining their USP—their **Unique Selling Proposition.** And it has nothing to do with price! Their USP is a clear and distinct differentiator for these businesses. They have spent time and effort perfecting what will make them different from their competition. They then focus their efforts on delivering their uniqueness. And when they do, people chose to buy from them time and time again.

So what is your Unique Selling Proposition? What is it that sets your business apart from your competitors? Have you thought it through? Are you delivering on that uniqueness every time you contact a client or customer?

Here's a homework assignment for you. Take 5 minutes, and write down EVERYTHING that sets you apart from your competition. List anything that comes to mind. What are you particularly good at? What makes your customers buy from you?

_____

_____

_____

_____

_____

_____

_____
_____
_____
_____
_____
_____
_____
_____
_____
_____
_____
_____

Now that you have a good list, put yourself in the mind of your competition and ask yourself, "Can I (as the competition) make the same statement or claim?" If the answer is yes, then strike that item off the list. If the answer is no, then leave that item on the list.

Once you are done, look at your list and find the items (if any) that have not been stricken off. These may just be the beginning of your USP!

If after this exercise, you have nothing on your list, then create a new list on a separate sheet of paper. Think harder about your business.

If you truly do not have anything that sets you apart, then now is the time to be creative and ask yourself "What could I do to set myself apart?" Start a list of potential future USPs. This may be the list that you will use to re-engineer your business and begin the process of defining your niche.

Make sense? If you have something that sets you apart, and it is something that your customers will value, then you are in great shape. Now all you have to do is execute that USP all the time!

If you come up empty, then be glad that you went through this exercise now because without a USP, you are sentenced to the slow death of competing on price, forever lowering your price, lowering your quality, lowering your service, and eventually shutting your business down. That's no way to win!

Assuming you have a list of qualities that distinguish you from your competition, write down your USP here:

_____

_____

_____

Once you have your USP, try it out on several of your customers. Get feedback from those you trust. Start mentioning it, delivering it, and highlighting it in your business.

If you can master this stage, you will set yourself up to not only have a sustainable business, but it will be profitable—and that is our ultimate goal.

STAGE 16
Establishing Your Guarantee

Welcome to Stage 16 of the Tour de Profit. I sincerely hope that you have found the first 15 stages to be both challenging and beneficial to your business. By now, you should be in a good rhythm. You should be thinking of each week as a new opportunity to lay a solid foundation on which to grow your business.

Challenging? Yes! Rewarding? Most certainly! Just know that most business owners will drop out of the race before it ends. They will lose focus, lose confidence, lose patience, and therefore, lose the race.

What about you? Are you committed to staying in the race all the way to Stage 52? If you are, finishing will be a huge accomplishment, and the best thing you could do for your business, and for your future.

In Stage 16, we are going to focus on your Guarantee. Yes, it is critical that every business has a Guarantee. If you do not have one yet, your assignment this week is to create a compelling one for your business. If you already offer a Guarantee, then your assignment this week is to enhance it, perfect it, and make sure you are gaining the benefit of having one.

So why is a Guarantee so important? The reality is that every business transaction has risk associated with it. In some cases the risk is obvious, and in others it is not so obvious. How you respond to the risks associated with your business will determine your reputation. There may be no greater asset in your business than your reputation.

Let me give you an example: If you take your shirts to a dry cleaner, there is a risk they will not be returned in a timely manner. There is also a risk that they will not be done the way you like them. Your shirts may be lost or given to another customer. The risks associated with a dry cleaner are not life threatening, but they will drive your decision on whether or not to use one dry cleaner over another.

So, if you are in the dry cleaning business, you need to determine what the most harmful risks are to your customers. Then ask yourself if you can give them a Guarantee that it will never happen at your dry cleaner.

Simply replace your business category for the dry cleaner, and answer the same question. What is the most serious or harmful risk in doing business in your industry, from the perspective of your customer? _____

_____

_____

_____

_____

_____

Now ask a second question, can you guarantee that it will never happen when doing business with you?

I know you can not guarantee that something will never happen. But don't let that stop you. Your Guarantee will assure your customers that if that terrible thing does occur, you are going to take total responsibility, and correct the situation in their favor.

Think of some of the most impactful Guarantees in business: Pizza delivered in 30 minutes or less—or it's FREE! Guaranteed delivery overnight by 10 am anywhere in the world! If you are not completely satisfied, you can return the empty bottle for a full refund!

Do you think a pizza was ever delivered later than 30 minutes? Sure! Do you think a package may have been late to its destination? No question about it! Have some customers returned a completely empty bottle and asked for a refund? Certainly! But the impact of having the guarantee has garnered more new business for these companies than they could have ever imagined.

Stop wringing your hands about the few who will "take advantage" of your Guarantee. Most business owners are paralyzed by the fear of a few nutcases who will scam you. Your fears are overstated. And you can structure your guarantee to minimize this risk to your business. Trust me, the rewards will make you forget the few who are looking for a free ride.

If you identify the risks potential customers face when doing business with you, and guarantee that those risks will not happen, your customers will appreciate doing business with you, and they will tell ten of their friends about you!

So what are you waiting for? Stage 16 is on. You've got your assignment. Take the time, think it through, ask your customers, and create a meaningful Guarantee that will drive more business to your doorstep!

STAGE 17
Marketing Plan on a Page

Did you get your assignment done last week? Are you now sporting a new and exciting Guarantee for your product or service? Have you tried it out on some of your loyal customers? What kind of feedback did you get? If you spent the time identifying the most concerning issue in your industry, and made your Guarantee addressing it, then you will have something that your customers will appreciate and value.

Now, we push forward! The Tour de Profit does not take a break. We get back on the bike each week—for 52 straight weeks—seeking to win each and every stage!

This is Stage 17. I consider this a "Time Trial" for the Tour de Profit. Your task is to create a One-Page Marketing Plan for your business.

This is a timed event. You will have 10 minutes for this time trial. No need for research. No need for you to talk with customers or prospective customers. Simply focus your efforts for 10 minutes, and create a One-Page Marketing Plan.

You've probably heard of Jay Conrad Levinson, the father of Guerrilla Marketing. Jay was also responsible for creating the Marlboro Man and taking Marlboro cigarettes from an unknown brand, to the number one brand in a short time. Now, I am not a fan of cigarettes, but I am a fan of using marketing strategies that work to grow your business. That is why I follow Jay Conrad Levinson, and practice many of his strategies. I think you should also.

This week's stage activity is straight from Jay Conrad Levinson's playbook. Rather than pay a marketing strategist a large sum to build a marketing strategy for your business, you are going to do it in 10 minutes! It may not be as pretty, with all of the bells and whistles that cost lots of money, but it will cover the seven critical areas that you must address to have a comprehensive marketing plan for your business.

To win this stage of the race, you need to set aside any other activity for the next ten minutes. Answer each of the next seven question in ten minutes. This is not an essay exam. This is about being direct, specific, and focused in your responses. I will ask each question a couple of different ways to help you get the right intent.

Are you ready to start the clock? GO!

#1 – What is the PURPOSE of your Marketing? In other words, what do you want someone to do PHYSICALLY when they know who you are and what you do? ____

_____

_____

_____

_____

_____

_____

_____

#2 – What is your COMPETITIVE ADVANTAGE? What sets you apart from your competition? _____

_____

_____

_____

_____

_____

_____

_____

#3 – Who is your TARGET MARKET? Who would be an ideal customer for your products or services? _____

_____

_____

_____

_____

_____

_____

_____

#4 – What MARKETING WEAPONS will you use? What strategies will you use to get people to know who you are and what you do? Here's a clue: your weapons in today's market must include extensive use of social media such as Facebook, LinkedIn, and others, as well as a well-managed Google presence. _____

_____

_____

_____

_____

_____

_____

#5 – What is your NICHE? Your Unique Selling Proposition? Why should people buy from you? _____

_____

_____

_____

_____

_____

_____

#6 – What is your IDENTITY? What is the personality of your business? _____

_____

_____

_____

_____

_____

_____

#7 – What is your BUDGET as a percentage of your gross sales? How much are you committing to invest on growing your business? _____

_____

_____

_____

_____

_____

_____

_____

That's it. You now have the essence of a marketing strategy for your business. You certainly have some details that need to be added, some specifics that would help make it even more clear and concise. Your answers to the questions above should give a template you can use to make marketing decisions—and get results!

Nicely done! Congratulations for focusing on what matters in your business.

STAGE 18
Defining the Business Chassis

Welcome to Stage 18 of this year's Tour de Profit! Believe it or not, this week marks the one-third point of the race. Only 34 stages left in the Tour. It is time to start pressing your advantage!

If you completed the last few stages well, you are positioned with a solid USP (Unique Selling Proposition), a meaningful Guarantee, and a Marketing Plan that will keep you focused on your primary message, and your target audience. Well done! These stages are critical to moving your business from price-only based competition to benefits-based competition.

In Stage 18 we will take advantage of your Niche and focus on the structure that supports growth in your business —what ActionCOACH calls your Business Chassis.

Notice the sequence of the Tour up to this point. It makes no sense to focus on growth if you have not clearly defined how you are differentiated from your competition. Many companies chose to focus only on growth, and they may get growth, but not the right kind of growth. It is critically important that you find your Niche first so that your growth can be PROFITABLE. If you missed the last few stages, go back and get those done before you begin to focus on your Business Chassis.

So just what is the Business Chassis? Every car has a chassis—the framework on which the car is built. In fact, many cars are built on the same or similar chassis. An example is the Ford Taurus and the Jaguar XJE. Both are built on the same chassis, yet one is built as a utility car that is reasonably priced, and the other is built as a well-appointed luxury car that is very expensive.

An average car and a high-performance car be built on the same chassis? Yes! The same is true for an average business and a high-performance business. Both are built on the same chassis. The difference comes from what the car builder, or business owner, does with the chassis. Some choose to build a high-performance machine with their chassis, while others don't understand the power that lies in their chassis; as a result, they build a modest, so-so machine.

The first step in building a high-performance business machine on your chassis is to understand the components of your chassis. You must know what you are working with, and how the components work together. Once you understand this, and focus on this, you will recognize the power that lies inside.

The Business Chassis is made up of five component parts. These are the five things that all businesses have in common. We all engage in these five activities, but many don't recognize that the activities are linked, and work together to provide the power to grow your business.

So let me give you an overview of the five components of the Business Chassis:

Generating Leads: All businesses generate leads to attract potential customers. Our ability to generate new leads is critical to our business success. The more, and better, leads we generate, the more exposure we get, and the more chances we have for selling our products or services.

Conversion Rate: All businesses take their leads through a process to convert them from a lead into a customer. Some lead conversion processes are very robust and well defined, others are haphazard and inconsistently performed. These conversion processes are typically known as our sales process.

Number of Transactions: All businesses can calculate the frequency of purchases for an average customer. In the case of a coffee shop, the frequency of purchases may be daily, while for a dentist, the frequency may be twice per year. The difference does not matter as much as the ability to know your frequency of purchases, and the strategies you use to increase that frequency.

Average $ Sale: All businesses have an average dollar amount for sales. Each time a customer makes a purchase, that purchase has a ticket price. Take the average of all purchases and calculate your average purchase price, or as I call it, your average "$" sale. Again, this number may vary widely depending upon the type of business, but what matters most is that you know what it is, and that you have a plan to increase it on a regular basis.

Profit Margin: All businesses have a profit margin for their products and services. Some may be greater than others. Some may even be in the negative. When you roll all your products and services together, you can calculate your average profit margin for your business. Once again, this will vary depending upon the business and industry. What matters most is that you know what yours is, and that you have a plan to improve it on a regular basis.

Your focus this week is to know the numbers for each aspect of your Business Chassis. If you haven't been tracking these numbers, this stage will take some time, but you can't progress on the Tour without concentrating on this stage.

Having the actual data for your business is important. Without it you will never know what is working and what is not.

Most business owners have a blind-fold on because they do not have the data on these five critical components of their business! It is like riding your bike with your eyes closed!

Get your data together this week and in our next stage, we will begin putting that data to work to build our high-performance business machine!

STAGE 19
Harnessing the Power of the Business Chassis

It is Stage 19 in your Tour de Profit. This is where the serious business owners will separate themselves from the pack.

Up to now, the race has been about positioning and setting yourself up for victory. But now we get down to the nuts and bolts of growing your business.

Last week, in Stage 18, I introduced the five key components of the Business Chassis: Generating Leads, Conversion Rate, Number of Transactions, Average $ Sale, and Profit Margin. Your assignment last week was to spend the time collecting the data necessary to know where your business is today in each of these key areas. How did you do? Were you able to collect and analyze your data to determine these answers?

If you did, then I want to congratulate you for your efforts, and your diligence, in keeping this kind of data on your business. Frankly, I know that the vast majority of business owners have no clue what these numbers mean to their business. It makes you ask the question, if these five areas are that critical to business, then why would someone be in business without knowing these numbers?

Let's first examine "why" these areas are so critical to your business. These five components are called the Business Chassis because your entire business "runs" on these components. No business operates without them. And, when you consider them as a mathematical equation, they represent the fundamental math that leads to business growth and success, or business failure and death.

Here's the math:

> Number of Leads Generated
> X Conversion Rate
> = Number of New Customers

If you intend to add more customers, you must do one of two things, or both:

1. You must increase your number of new leads (those who are aware that your business exists).

2. Increase your effectiveness in converting those leads into customers.

Both can be done, but both require specific strategies to make your efforts effective and productive. The math looks like this:

> Number of Customers
> X Number of Transactions (frequency of purchase)
> X Average $ Sale (average ticket price)
> = Total Revenues

Once you know your **total number of customers**, then you can multiply that number by their **average purchase frequency** to get the **total number of transactions** you should expect in a period. Then, multiply that number by the **average sale**, and you get the **total revenues generated** during that period.

If you want to increase your revenues, you must either:

- Increase the frequency of purchase of your existing customers.

- Get them to buy more each time they visit you.

Again, both paths are achievable, but both will require different strategies to get the results you want.

Once you have your **new total revenues**, you can multiply that by your **profit margin** to get your **total available margin, or operating profit**.

If you want to increase the profitability of your business, then you must find ways to improve your profit margins, so that you make additional margin dollars on each and every transaction.

Again, there are several strategies that will work to make this happen. You simply must decide what you are going to accomplish, and implement the strategies in a focused manner.

Now, here is where the magic comes in:

Leads Generated

X Conversion Rate

X Number of Transactions

X Average $ Sale

X Profit Margins

= **PROFITS**

Because this is a math equation, each individual component is magnified in it's importance because of the multiplicative effect. In other words, since each component is multiplied by the others, even a small change in every component can result in a large change in the bottom line profit.

For example, a 10% increase in each of the five components of the Business Chassis will result in a **62%** increase in the bottom line profits! Small improvements focused on each of these five areas will have a dramatic increase in your business. Sound too good to be true? It is real—trust me!

This is a powerful concept that most business owners overlook. Simply understanding how the math equation works is game changing, and taking the time to develop the specific strategies to make the improvement can change the course of your business.

In the upcoming stages we will examine each of the five components in detail, and outline opportunities for improvements in your business. This week, get the concept clear in your head. Try out the math on a piece of paper. Do some "what if's," and prove to yourself that there is truly power in the Business Chassis. Then, we'll begin putting meat on the bones in Stages 20 thru 24 during what I call the Mountain Stages.

Ride well and ride strong this week. The Mountain Stages ahead will require your focus and commitment!

MOUNTAIN REGION

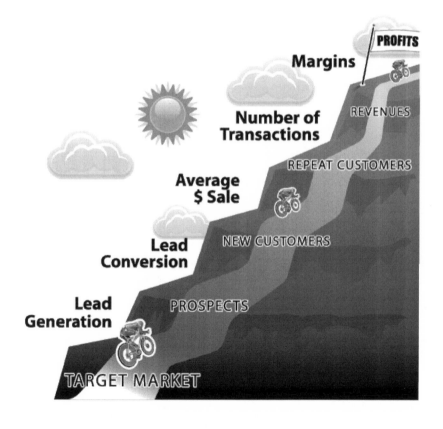

STAGE 20
Lead Generation

I hope you did well in last week's stage where we discussed the power that exists in understanding your Business Chassis. If you applied the math to your current situation, you no doubt realized that by focusing on five specific areas of your business, you could dramatically change the performance and profitability of your business. Most business owners don't realize the power of this simple system. You are at an advantage in this race.

In this week's stage of the Tour de Profit, we will be focused on the first of five Mountain Stages. Why do I call these the Mountain Stages? Because only the strongest riders in the Tour de Profit will have what it takes to not only survive these stages, but also win them. This is truly where the rubber meets the road. Watch what happens over these next five weeks!

The first peak is named lead generation. Without lead generation, your business will flounder, and ultimately fail. Superior lead generation requires a well thought out plan, a commitment to be consistent, and a coordinated effort between your different lead generation strategies.

The first step, in this stage, is to go back to your notes from Stage 17 where you outlined your marketing plan. You must be very clear on your purpose, your competitive advantages, your target markets, your niche, and your budget when making your plan for generating leads for your business.

Once you have your plan firmly in mind, step two is to identify eight to ten strategies you will use to get those in your target market to know that you exist.

As you are listing your specific strategies, make sure to allocate at least one or two specific strategies to your social media and online presence. You may not be sure how you are going to implement these particular strategies, but if you want to set yourself apart from your competition and prepare your business for the future, you MUST begin the journey into the world of Google, Facebook, LinkedIn, and social media.

List your eight to ten strategies here:

1. _____

2. _____

3. _____

4. _____

5. _____

6. _____

7. _____

8. _____

9. _____

10. _____

These specific lead generation strategies are like the spokes on the front wheel of your bike. If you only have one or two, your wheel is not very stable. Likewise, if you are trying to grow your business using only one or two lead generation strategies, your results will likely be erratic and unpredictable.

There is also no need for too many spokes on your front wheel. Likewise, you do not need to spread your efforts across too many lead generation strategies. Be selective— eight to ten to start.

Allocate your marketing budget between these specific strategies. I am not recommending that you invest more money in lead generation. Simply allocate what you have budgeted for marketing (lead generation). Once you start collecting data on your results, you can adjust your allocation to those strategies that work better than others.

Next, make a commitment to how many repetitions you are going to do in each lead generation strategy. For instance, If you have included direct mail as one of your strategies, how many mailings are you going to send each week? If you are going to use networking as one of your strategies, how many new contacts (leads) are you going to make each week? If you are going to do cold-calling or bold walk-in's, how many are you going to do weekly? How many new prospects are you going to add to your list of those who know you? Be specific. Set a goal. Do the work necessary to win.

A critical commitment you must make in this stage is to MEASURE your results and TEST any adjustments you make. The best way to create an effective and efficient lead generation machine is:

- To have the discipline to make a plan
- Stick to the plan
- Do the required repetitions
- Measure the results from your efforts
- Make changes one at a time, so you can test and measure what happens when you change one of the variables

As you experience positive results in one or more of your lead generation strategies, allocate more time, effort and resources to those that work.

If you find some do not work well, make adjustments, test the results of the change, and either continue to tweak them, or, at some point, eliminate them from your plan. Over time, you will identify the six to eight strategies that work best for you and your business.

I assure you, if you apply discipline to this element of the Business Chassis, you will set yourself apart from your competition—by a wide margin. While your competition is all over the map, trying to make something work, you will be working your plan, executing your plan, and measuring your plan. You will be making improvements based on the data you collect, and, over time, far outperforming every-one in your marketplace.

Next week, we will focus on your Lead Conversion activities. But first, get your homework done for this stage.

It is a Mountain Stage, so expect it the "burn" before you reach the end of the week. Remember the prize you are chasing—winning the Tour de Profit. You will thank yourself later for pushing hard through this stage.

STAGE 21
Converting Leads into Customers

Welcome to Stage 21 of the Tour de Profit! It is hard to believe that we are 20 weeks into the course. How time flies when you are growing your business!

In this stage, we are going to focus on making the absolute most of the work you did in Stage 20, building your machine for generating leads.

One of the biggest tragedies is watching a business owner spend significant time and effort generating leads for a business, but then not converting those leads into paying customers. I'll bet you know someone who has a stack of business cards on their desk that they have collected, but they have not added those cards to their customer database. No follow up has taken place, and the business cards are growing colder by the day.

If this is getting a little too close to home, it is time to get out of the trap, and start turning those leads into paying customers. Wouldn't you agree?

To make improvements in this stage, you simply have to start doing one thing: MEASURE your current conversion success rate!

Most business owners have no clue what their conversion rate is. By simply measuring where you are, you will improve. Add to that a specific, focused approach to handling your leads, and your conversion rate will go through the roof!

The best part is, you can grow your business without spending one more dollar! You've already invested marketing dollars to generate the leads. Now, make the most of that investment by defining your specific, repeatable sales steps that will convert your leads into customers.

To get started, take a few minutes to write down the specific steps that you take every lead through to get them familiar with you and your business. Each business has a different set of steps in their selling process. Some have just a few steps; others have many steps. You must decide how familiar a new prospect needs to be with you, and your business, in order to pull out their wallet and make a purchase.

_____

_____

_____

_____

_____

_____

_____

_____

_____

Now that you have your current process steps written down, ask yourself, "Is everyone in your business following the process?" If not, why not? How can you have a "best in class" approach if you allow each individual to "roll their own"? How can you test and measure new approaches if you don't have a standard? How can you improve and predict outcomes if there are multiple approaches?

I often hear business owners say they would lose their best sales people if they made them follow a standard sales process. Let me ask you, whose business is it? Who has all the risk in the deal? Who is setting the expectations and limitations? My hope is that it is you, the business owner. Don't let the personal preferences of others dictate how you will run your business, unless you like working *for* them!

The best way to accomplish this Mountain Stage is to have the discipline to follow these steps:

- Establish your specific selling process steps
- Train your team to follow the selling process
- Support it with the necessary materials
- Measure the results of each specific step
- Make changes to your sales process based on the results of your measurements.
- Test and Measure
- Test and Measure
- Test and Measure
- Make incremental improvements
- Hold yourself and your team accountable for the results

There is a point in your sales process where your prospect will do something physical to indicate they are ready to buy. If you can identify that "physical something" for your business, then point all of your efforts to make that happen, your conversion rate will improve.

I call this the "get on the boat" moment. One of my clients has a 100-person catamaran on which he holds corporate events, private parties, wedding, etc. His specific physical something for his prospects is to get them to step on his boat. Once they do that, they are so impressed that they are very likely to sign a contract.

What is your "get on the boat" moment? Write it down here: _____

_____

Make sure your team knows this moment.

Stage 21 is a tough, yet rewarding, Mountain Stage. If you can master it, you will separate yourself from your competition.

Many will not do well climbing this stage. They will falter, and go back to their old ways of doing business. Don't let this happen to you. Stay focused. Be determined. Build a repeatable process for converting leads into customers. Your business success will become a certainty.

STAGE 22
Increasing Frequency of Purchase

We are entering Stage 22 where your task is to focus on how you increase the frequency of purchase by your customers. This is the third component of the Business Chassis. We've covered the first two: Lead Generation and Lead Conversion. These stages focused on getting more customers. Now, it is time to focus on making the most of the customers you already have, and those you now are gaining.

Remember, we are in the Mountain Stages of the Tour de Profit. These are the most grueling challenges in the 52-stage race, but they are also the stages that will separate you from your competition. Most of your competitors have no clue what the Business Chassis is all about. They don't understand the power that comes from the multiplicative nature of the five key components of the Business Chassis.

I remind you of this so you will not lose focus. I want you to stay engaged and determined to win these difficult stages in the race. These Mountain Stages take determination and will power, but the rewards are great. Keep pressing forward; you are making great progress!

Now, let's focus on frequency of purchase. Do you know what the average frequency of purchase is for your business? If you don't know find it now. Then start tracking it over the next weeks.

How often does the average customer buy from you in a year? I realize there is a wide range, from those who buy only once, to those who may buy monthly, weekly or even daily. However, there is an average.

Simply take all your transactions in the period and divide them by the number of unique customers you have served in that same period. That is your average purchase frequency. If you do not know it, take a few minutes right now to calculate it.

You may ask, why is this so important? As one of the five key components of the Business Chassis, this is a critical metric in the growth of your business. Not only does it matter, but, here's the kicker, increasing the frequency of purchase of your current customers is the most cost effective way to increase your revenues and profits!

Think about it! You don't have to sell them on doing business with you; they already like doing business with you. You don't have to spend money trying to find them; you already have them in your database. You don't have to pay a fee to get their contact data; you already have it. You don't even have to educate them on the benefits of doing business with you; you have already done that.

Since it is so easy to sell to someone who is already doing business with you, already likes you, already understands your value, why do you spend the majority of your time prospecting for new customers?

What are you doing to get those who already do business with you to simply do MORE business with you? Are you afraid you will bug them or scare them off? Are you not proud of your product or service? Are you not confident that you offer the best value proposition in your industry?

I often tell the story of a florist in a small town. She heard me talk about increasing the frequency of purchase from her existing customers, and the light bulb went on in her head. She sent a note to all of her existing customers inviting them to do something different for Father's Day. Just by simply reminding her current customers of what she had to offer on a special day, she had her biggest Father's Day weekend in sales. And it did not cost her one-dime! She simply invited her current customers to come back one more time.

How many times is too many? The answer depends upon how confident you are that your product or service. If it is the best (as it should be) then why not be proud of it, and remind your customers frequently? If you are not that confident, then you have work to do!

Do your customers know everything you offer? Are they currently buying your complete range of products or services? Are there other offerings that may also work for them?

The strategies for increasing your frequency of purchase are endless. You could give your customers a time-sensitive offer when they make a purchase. You can create a frequent purchase program. Quickly jot down as many ideas as you can for increasing frequency of purchase:

_____

_____

_____

_____

_____

_____

_____

Communicate more frequently with your customers. Invite them to come back again and again. Don't be shy. They will let you know if you are going overboard. You will likely be more sensitive about the frequency of contact with them than they are, particularly if you consistently deliver great value.

Good luck on this stage. It is a Mountain Stage because only the strong and determined will follow through. The rest will read this chapter, file it away, and do nothing only to complain later that they need more customers. Don't fall into that trap! Invite your customers to visit you more often!

STAGE 23
Raising Your Average Dollar Sale

Are you ready for the next Mountain Stage in the Tour de Profit. In Stage 23, we will explore the fourth element of the Business Chassis: Average $ Sale. In this stage, we improve revenues and profits by focusing on each and every customer you have, and giving them the opportunity to buy something extra every time they do business with you.

Many call this the McDonald's approach. "Would you like fries with that?" Ever hear that phrase? Ever wonder why they asked that question? Did you think they were trying to drive you crazy? No, they have a plan. They have a motive. They know that a certain percentage of customers would answer that question with "sure." As a result, they increase their revenues without ever gaining one single new customer.

Look around you. Businesses are doing it everywhere. You can't get out of a grocery store, a Home Depot or

Lowe's, or Target without first "running the gauntlet" of candy, magazine, snacks, gum, batteries, lip gloss, you name it. What do you think the impact of having those "impulse" items available, and accessible, would be when they have 1,000 people go through the check out every day? If 1,000,000 people simply added $1 to their sale, the additional revenue would be $1,000,000.

So you have to ask, if an extra dollar on each sale means so much to a big company, why doesn't it mean as much to smaller ones? How do you think big companies got that way? They used every opportunity to add to each and every sale.

Are you following their example? If not, what would it take for you to identify your "fries with that" items? _____

_____

_____

_____

_____

_____

_____

_____

Let me share a real example I encountered recently. I had the opportunity to vacation on the North Shore of Lake Superior. We were spending a wonderfully relaxing time in Two Harbors, MN, taking a break from the August heat in Texas. One afternoon we made our way to one of the true Minnesota icons, Betty's Pies. We had been to Betty's Pies before, and considered it a required stop.

As is usual in the summer, Betty's Pies was packed, even at 3:00 pm on a Monday afternoon. After a wait, we were seated and immediately greeted by our waitress, Mary Marker. Mary was the living picture of "Minnesota Nice"; she made us feel right at home. Her service was outstanding, and we were truly enjoying our time.

As we finished our late lunch, Mary came by our table and confidently asked, "What kind of pie will you be having today?" Now, my standard response to a question about dessert is "no thanks." However, while we were taken back by her presumption that we wanted dessert, her approach and enthusiasm left us with no option other than to respond with "the Great Lakes Crumb, please." The result was an immediate increase in our ticket price of $7.98!

Mary had nailed the concept of asking if we wanted "fries with that." In fact, she did it even one better. As soon as I gave her my choice of pie, she responded with, "Do you want that warmed with ice cream?" Who could say no! Of course, I wanted my pie served warm with ice cream. The result? Yet another $0.95 to the ticket price!

Our lunch ticket before Mary asked about dessert was $23.04. After Mary's effective approach of adding value to our meal, our lunch ticket was $31.97—a whopping 38% increase in our ticket price!

Not only was the pie the best you could find, but I was intrigued by Mary's natural approach to increasing the average ticket price of every customer she waited on.

Do your team members behave like Mary at Betty's Pies? Having "fries with that" items available isn't enough. Your team needs to not only be aware of the offer, but to also be offering it to every customer. How ingrained is the offer in your sales script?

Do you make it easy to "up-sell" your customers? Do you bundle your products and services? If you did, the result would be a higher average ticket price! There are many strategies you can use to increase your average ticket price. Remember, you don't need to raise it by a large amount. Simply a 10% increase from, say, $250 to $275 would have a significant impact on your revenues, not to mention your profits.

So, your challenge this week is short and sweet. Think through the many ways you can get each customer to buy just a little more, every time they do business with you. Some methods will work well, others not so much. Measure your results and test the outcomes. Be deliberate in your approach until you find the magic combination of add-ons, upgrades, or bundles.

Remember, each element of the Business Chassis builds upon the others, so every little movement matters in a big way. Take small steps, but be consistent. Build routine into your expectations. Do what McDonald's and other large, successful businesses do: make "fries with that" a part of how you do business. The results will astound you, and your bottom line will be better off for it!

Here's to your success in Stage 23. Congratulations for working hard!

STAGE 24
Improving Your Profit Margins

Stage 24 is the last of the five Mountain Stages. This week, we complete the Business Chassis by focusing on your Profit Margins.

Over the past four weeks, you have worked on Lead Generation, Lead Conversion, increasing the Number of Transactions, and increasing your Average Dollar Sale. Each of these, by themselves, is a significant driver of growth, and profitability, in any business. Together, they represent the most powerful combination of elements that can truly change the trajectory of your business. The power comes from the multiplicative effect these have on your financials.

This week, we will focus on your Profit Margins. You can have a fast growing business, but without acceptable profit margins, all of your growth will be for nothing.

It is critically important that you not only know your overall margins, but you must also know them by product or service type.

Why is this so important? Because you want to be sure you are promoting and selling your highest margin products and services whenever you can. These are the game-changers for you. These products and services are the ones that cover your costs and provide you with resources to invest in your business.

There are two primary ways you can improve the Profit Margins in your business:

1. Reduce your expenses

2. Raise your prices.

Most cringe at the thought of raising prices, especially in today's fragile market, but, if you have done the hard work of creating a Unique Selling Position, and have truly differentiated yourself from your competition, raising your prices may be an option.

Usually the fear of raising prices is based on the unknown response from your customers. But, studies have shown that your loyal customers are not doing business with you simply because of price. They appreciate your USP, and will remain loyal customers as long as you have treated them well and found ways to deliver more than they expected.

Cutting costs is often easier, but not necessarily the right move to make when you are trying to grow your company. Eliminating waste is always good, but often expense cutting comes in the form of eliminating services, reducing staff, and degrading your ability to deliver on your promises. Be careful not to impact your operational efficiency and speed of delivery when reducing your expenses. The last thing you want to do is to become a "me too" business because of your efforts to cut costs.

With that caution in mind, there are always ways to gain efficiency and reduce the effective cost of your system. Toyota, and other large manufacturing companies, particularly those based in Japan, have mastered cost cutting through waste reduction, efficiency, reduced work in process inventories, and unnecessary movement of people and supplies. If they can do it, so can you.

When was the last time you critically evaluated your business operations with an eye towards gaining efficiencies and reducing unnecessary steps in your process? This is a powerful way to reduce your costs while improving your productivity and customer satisfaction.

The challenge is to first know your margins, then be purposeful in improving them on a regular basis. The trend for your margins should always be favorable. Work hard on this last segment of the Business Chassis, and you will position yourself for phenomenal growth and incredible profits. Not a bad outcome for the effort involved!

Good luck on this Stage 24. Finish strong in this Mountain Stage, and you will find yourself in the winner's circle!

LEVERAGE
REGION

STAGE 25
Shifting Gears Through Leverage

Let me be the first to congratulate you for making it through the difficult Mountain Stages of the Tour de Profit! I hope you took the time to do the work that was required to complete these five stages: Lead Generation, Lead Conversion, Frequency of Purchase, Average Sale Price, and Profit Margins. If you took a short cut over these past five weeks, and did not do your homework, you will certainly be sorry. Not to mention you will have missed out on one of the most powerful concepts you will ever come across for growing your business.

You've been doing well on this race, but now is not the time to rest or take a break. As we near the halfway point in this 52-stage race, much lays ahead. Acknowledge how far you've come, and the rewards you've generated, but also prepare for what's ahead.

It is now time to enter yet another challenging, but rewarding, region on the tour. Today we begin Stage 25 and enter the region called Leverage. This is an exciting, four-stage region where you have the opportunity to "shift gears" and get yourself out of the monotonous day-to-day routines of your business.

Shifting gears is a good thing. If you were to try to ride this entire race in a single gear, there would be times when you would be literally spinning your wheels, and other times when you would have to get off your bike to push it up a hill. Gears play a critical role on a bike; in business, leverage means getting more done by working less!

Now, if I told you that I could help you put out less effort and accomplish more each day, would that be of interest to you? I hope so! If you think the idea of working ever more efficiently, and getting ever more done, is a concept that would work for you, then let's get after it!

Let me set up these next four stages of the race by giving you an overview of the Leverage Region. There are four areas of your business where you can apply leverage in a meaningful and impactful way:

1. The processes you use to get work done

2. The marketing strategies you use to promote your business

3. The people processes you apply to your business

4. The technology you bring to bear in your business.

Each of these four areas holds a gold mine of improvement that can be gained through leverage.

Let me give you a few examples to get your juices flowing. Think about any area of your business where you repeat the same steps on a regular basis. This can be in the sales process, in your manufacturing processes, in your quality control area, in your finance department, your purchasing function, or your human resources activities. Anywhere you have activities that are done on a repeated basis there are opportunities to improve through leverage.

Think about those areas in your business where you have multiple people doing the same task, such as sales, order entry, assembly operations, packaging and shipping, delivery, or accounts payable. These are prime suspects for improvement through leverage.

Do a mental list of those areas of your business where you could use technology to help streamline a task, improve the speed of processing, reduce the variation, or eliminate waste. Each of these areas is a good target for applying leverage in your business.

So here is your challenge for the week. Get your wheels spinning by creating a list of all of the repeatable activities in your business.

_____

_____

_____

_____

_____

_____

_____

_____

_____

_____

_____
_____
_____
_____
_____
_____
_____
_____
_____

Now prioritize these activities. Give yourself 100 points. Look over your entire list, and apply some number of points to those items on the list that you think would have the biggest impact on the success, or efficiency, of your business.

If you have something on your list that is interesting but not that critical, then do not assign any points to that item. If there is another activity that is mission critical, assign it a high point value. Allocate your 100 points among your list, with at least 10 items receiving some points. Organize these from highest to lowest.

1. _____
2. _____
3. _____
4. _____
5. _____
6. _____
7. _____
8. _____
9. _____
10. _____

These will be what you will focus on over the next four weeks.

Are you ready? This is not difficult work, but it is game changing. Remember, your competitors aren't doing it, so why not take this opportunity to distance yourself from them. While they are resting, and thinking nothing will change, you will be re-inventing your business from the inside out—and quickly distancing yourself from the rest of the pack.

OK, get to work. Stage 25 is underway. Do the baseline work this week, and we'll dive into the specifics of creating Leverage through out your business next week.

STAGE 26
Building Leverage into Your Processes

Welcome to Stage 26 of the Tour de Profit! We have entered the Leverage Region, and, for the next four weeks, we will be focused on how to gain an advantage on our competition through Leverage.

This week's stage is specifically focused on building Leverage into your day-to-day operational processes. There's a lot to cover, so let's get right to it.

First, look over your homework from last week. Remember, we discussed thinking about your business and prioritizing those repeatable activities that occur in your business. We want to be sure that we focus our attention first on the areas of your business that will provide you the biggest bang for your buck. From last week's activities, you should have a good feel for the repeating activities that are most critical to your business success.

Let's concentrate on the activities that make up your day-to-day business operations. These should be the ones that matter most to your customers. Why? Because how you handle the day-to-day operations of your business defines who you are, and what your value is to your customers. For instance, if you are in the Dry Cleaning business, how you take in dirty laundry is a critical repeatable process. You have to count the items, know what type of starch that particular customer prefers, record that you have their clothing, and provide a receipt—all within a matter of minutes.

If you are in the restaurant business, you need to greet your customers in a certain way, determine their preferred seating arrangements, handle the menu, and take their order. How you handle these activities will set a tone and a "feeling" for your restaurant. Can you imagine handling each customer differently? Without the certainty of the process, how can you think about creating a brand or feeling?

Let's agree that for each and every process in your business, there is a "best" way to get the process done. Why not, then, have everyone do that same process the same "best" way?

I find that most business owners who have a few long-term team members are the least structured and organized in this area. Why? Because they have become reliant on their long-term employees and their know-how to handle situations. So what happens when they are on vacation, out sick, or, worse yet, leave unexpectedly? As the business owner, you must own the processes and own the documentation that supports the processes.

Now, before you shut down, and walk away from the idea of putting your processes on paper, let me tell you that this is the first step to building true Leverage in your business. Only when you have activity steps written down, so that everyone on your team knows what is expected, and everyone is trained on doing the tasks, will you have built Leverage into your business.

Here are some of the more common day-to-day processes you should document, post, and train your folks on:
- Receiving inventory
- Ordering supplies
- Greeting customers
- Cleaning the shop
- Preparing raw materials
- Taking inventory
- Processing expenses
- Shipping orders
- Re-stocking shelves
- Completing applications
- Responding to inquiries
- Recording daily progress
- Etc., etc.

The list can go on forever!

One of my clients made the decision to write out the step-by-step processes for every activity in his workplace. Then, he had the document laminated and posted, so that it was visible to everyone where the work was done. Now there is no need for him to tell, and re-tell, his team how he wants things done. He doesn't have to spend a lot of time training the new team members. He simply shows them what to look for, tells them to ask questions if there is something they do not understand, and off they go. He spends way less time worrying about the outcomes, because he knows the results he gets when his team follows the process. As a bonus, his customers see him as a very organized, fully functional business!

So, do you want some of that for your business? If so, start documenting your process steps. Start with the most critical day-to-day activities in your business. Set the tone for not only WHAT you want done, but HOW you expect it to get done. Meanwhile, you will be gaining leverage through your processes in ways that your competition will never understand or appreciate.

You're off! Time to get started turning your day-to-day activities into highly—leveraged processes. Trust me, you will be glad you worked hard during this stage of the race!

STAGE 27
Creating Highly Leveraged Marketing Strategies

It is hard to believe, but we are at the halfway point of the Tour de Profit! Take a quick look over your shoulder. How are you feeling about the race so far? Is your plan still in tact, and are you on pace to exceed your goals? If not, now is the time to dust off your plans and re-set your activities.

This week, we enter Stage 27 where your challenge is to create highly-leveraged marketing strategies within your business. As you recall, in this Leverage Region of the race, we are focused on areas of the business where we can do the work once. That's the definition of Leverage.

This week, we are shifting our focus to our Marketing Strategies. If you want to have consistent messaging and exposure for your business, you need to make your marketing efforts repeatable and self-sustaining.

I know this has never happened to you, but let me give you a typical scenario:

A business owner spends a significant amount of time marketing and promoting their business, only to be so successful that they land several new customers. Their workload increases, and soon they focus the majority of their time fulfilling their new customers orders. Meanwhile, they are not doing much marketing and promoting.

After a short period of time, the business owner looks up to find their business is slowing down, so they go back out and market heavily once again. Again, they secure more business, become overwhelmed, and focus on delivering their product or service to the customer. Once again, without the consistent marketing, the new business slows down and they find themselves in a repeating cycle.

In Stage 19, you developed six to eight strategies to expand awareness of your business. It's time to look at those strategies anew. Ask yourself how each marketing strategy could work on a consistent basis without you having to personally be involved. Come up with three or four ideas for each strategy.

Strategy 1: _____

       1. _____

       2. _____

       3. _____

       4. _____

Strategy 2: _____

       1. _____

       2. _____

       3. _____

       4. _____

Strategy 3: _____

      1. _____

      2. _____

      3. _____

      4. _____

Strategy 4: _____

      1. _____

      2. _____

      3. _____

      4. _____

Strategy 5: _____

      1. _____

      2. _____

      3. _____

      4. _____

Strategy 6: _____

      1. _____

      2. _____

      3. _____

      4. _____

Strategy 7: _____

        1. _____

        2. _____

        3. _____

        4. _____

Strategy 8: _____

        1. _____

        2. _____

        3. _____

        4. _____

If you are the only one who knows how that particular strategy works, then one of your actions will be to document the step-by-step processes you take to do it. If you consistently do a mailing, or run an advertisement, how can you systematize it so that the mailings get sent, or the ad gets placed on a regular basis?

In some cases, you may need to involve team members, or assign specific activities to someone outside of your business. For instance, if you are doing search engine optimization, but are relying on your personal skills in this area, ask yourself, "Is my time better utilized optimizing my SEO, or meeting with prospects and landing new customers?"

I often see business owners who are personally involved in the execution of their marketing strategies, rather than focusing their efforts on meeting new prospects and landing new clients. Why? Maybe it's because it is easier for them to focus on marketing strategies. Maybe they don't like doing the "selling" of their business.

You need to determine where your efforts are optimally used in your business. Once you find that, focus, and put systems in place to handle the other activities.

Businesses that leverage their marketing are more likely to maintain a consistent flow of new prospects and new customers. Their business growth occurs more predictably than those who turn the marketing faucet on and off.

Which type of business would you rather have? One that is consistently growing, or one that is constantly up and down?

Work hard this week on Stage 27. Your business will not only benefit, but your growth will also become more consistent and predictable.

STAGE 28
People Processes that Create Leverage

Welcome to Stage 28 of the Tour de Profit! This week you will be building Leverage into your business through People Processes. A powerful way to Leverage your time and resources is to work with the best people in your industry. Adding the right people to your team, training your team to be the best in their category, and motivating your team to do better is a huge challenge. But to win a race, you need a good support team.

Dr. Deming, the world-renowned quality guru once said that 94% of all failures in business are the result of "systems," and only 6% of the failures are caused by the people. Yet, when things go wrong, we often begin by look at the people involved to "find the guilty party."

If we were honest with ourselves, we would have to admit that the guilty party is most often the business owner. We are the ones who are asking our people to work in a "system" that is not clearly defined, without written processes, with faulty equipment, and, often, without sufficient guidance or direction.

So let's focus on building a better "system" that will both improve the consistency of output and gain us Leverage at the same time.

When it comes to the people side of the business, the best place to start is your hiring process. What is your hiring process? Is it repeatable? Is it reliable? Can you be certain that you will make the best hiring decision? You need to be able to answer "absolutely" to each question!

Most hiring processes waste a great deal of people's time—yours, your team's, and your job applicants. Think differently about how you make hiring decisions, and your process will surely change.

For instance, why not streamline your hiring process by implementing a hiring "system" that will allow you to screen multiple candidates in a consistent manner in a matter of hours? I can assure you that you will find the process more fulfilling, you will spend less time, your results will be more consistent, and your job candidates will appreciate it.

How about the personal development and skills training for your team? Does every person on your team have his or her own personal development plan? Are they taking responsibility and ownership for expanding their skills and improving themselves? Are you holding them accountable to read, learn, and apply new skills? Make learning and skill development a job expectation. Your team members will thank you as they become more capable and more confident in their ability to do the job they have been assigned.

Think about your performance assessment process. How do you give feedback to your team members? Do you have a structured approach, or is your approach more hit-or-miss? Do you encourage your team members to give feedback to each other in a constructive way?

Instead of taking all the responsibility for reviews and performance feedback, leverage your resources by asking everyone to participate in the process. Constructive feedback from peers is often the most effective way to get people to change their behaviors.

These are just a few of the "systems" you can put in place to gain Leverage from your People Processes. Incremental changes in this area can result in not only huge time-savings, but also increased performance and job satisfaction. Take your People Processes seriously. Involve your team in the solutions.

Your task in this stage is to make incremental improvements in your People Processes. Put at least one new process in place this week to improve your business team. Make a change, then measure and test.

Good luck this week! You're having a good ride. Stay focused, and you will win Stage 28!

STAGE 29
Using Technology to Gain Efficiency

This week, we are going to tackle the final stage of the Leverage Region. Stage 29 is focused on using technology to improve efficiencies and consistencies in your business. This is an important stage in building leverage, both in the impact that technology can have on your processes, and the investment required to introduce technology into your system. Because of the importance and impact, you must pay close attention and focus this week!

Let me be clear that technology is not always the best answer to improving the processes in a business. In fact, the implementation of technology can often be the absolute wrong thing to do for a business. If you are considering investing in technology, it is critical that you have a clear view of where you want to go, and why the technology is necessary.

Many business owners look to technology first, rather than doing everything possible to improve processes without using technology. When the technology solution is introduced too early, the outcome often "locks in" a bad process.

Think about it for a minute. When you use technology, you are often simply hard-wiring the process that is currently used. What if the process that is being used has not been optimized? What if there are flaws in your current processes? What if your processes are not as efficient as they should be? If any of these situations are true, then you are simply hard-wiring those flaws and inefficiencies into your business.

Instead of starting with the technology first, I suggest you spend time mapping out your current processes. I prefer doing this with a team of people using sticky notes to document each step of your process on a wall. Make sure that you have many different perspectives of the process. Then, ask everyone to step back from the wall of sticky notes and begin to identify all of the areas where the process is:

- Currently inefficient
- Has obvious waste
- Where delays occur
- Where costs are too high
- Where too many people are required
- Etc.

Work from your sticky note wall to re-design your process first. Allow everyone to share his or her views, opinions, perspectives, and suggestions. Take everything into account. Don't think you know everything—because often you do not. Bringing a good cross-section of people into your process mapping exercise (perhaps even a customer or supplier as well) will ensure their buy-in and acceptance of any changes that get made.

My experience has proven that if you go through this exercise first, you will always find a better way to do what you are currently doing, no matter what part of your business or service you examine.

Once you have identified improvements, take the time to "prove them out." Not weeks and months. Do it quickly before the enthusiasm for the effort goes away. Again, this hands-on approach will no doubt uncover some additional tweaks and changes to your processes.

Only after you have gone through these steps should you entertain the thought of a technology solution. Remember, once you make the investment in technology, you will be "living" with your decision for a long time, if for no other reason than the amount of money you invested into the technology.

With your new process map in hand, you are in a better position to know exactly what functions and features you will need in your technology solution. You will be able to measure the outcomes more effectively, and will know the outcomes with more certainty. At this point, the use of technology can move you ahead of your competition by leaps and bounds. Don't shy away from considering technology, but do it knowing there is significant up-front work to get the results you are expecting.

So here is your assignment for this stage:

1. Find one of the critical processes in your business that you believe could be a game-changer if you introduced a technology improvement.

2. Gather the key players who are familiar with this process into a Process Mapping session.

3. Map the current process on the wall using sticky notes.

4. Identify improvements that can and should be made.

5. Test the new process ideas over a period of a couple of days.

6. Revise the process map.

7. Use the new process map as your specification tool for the technology solution.

Go through this sequence at least once. I guarantee that you will find there are huge opportunities in the improvements even before you apply technology!

Technology solutions can set you apart, but you must follow a protocol to insure you are making a wise investment, and not simply a hasty expenditure.

STAGE 30
Creating a Memory with your Family

We're over halfway through the Tour de Profit. You've just completed the race stages that helped you create Leverage in your business. So there is no more appropriate time to take a well-deserved rest.

Stage 30 is an off-week. No racing; no working on the business this week. This week is reserved for creating a memory with your family. You work hard. You sacrifice on a regular basis. You often miss significant events or activities. You can't do it all. Frustrating?

You say how important your family is to you, but then you put in long, difficult hours at work. What is the message you are actually sending to your family? Take this week to prove what is most important to you. If you want to make sure your actions reflect what you say, this week is for you!

Creating a memory does not require a large cash outlay. It does not require three months of planning. It does not demand a complicated travel schedule. It simply requires that you put some thought into what your special people would love to do. What would catch them off guard? What could you do with them that would have them talking for weeks and months?

Need an idea? Confide in a friend. Let them know what you're trying to do, and they will give you some great ideas. Brainstorm five or six great ideas with your friend.

1. _____

2. _____

3. _____

4. _____

5. _____

6. _____

From this list, you will find something you can do with the special people in your life that is both doable and memorable.

If this were about your business, you would do it! So what is keeping you from having the same focus with your family? Nothing! Coordinate something that will make you proud of yourself, tell your family you love them, and create a memory for them.

Have fun! Remember to take photos! You'll want to look back to this week when things get tough. Don't miss this opportunity to be someone's super hero!

TEAM
REGION

STAGE 31
The 7 Keys to a Winning Team

This week we enter another important region on the Tour. This is the Team Region. In this series of weeks, we will highlight the Seven Keys to creating a Winning Team.

There may be nothing more important to the success of your business than your team. They encompass everything about your business:

- How work gets done
- How relationships get formed
- How culture is defined
- How celebrations are made
- How businesses are built.

I've seen business owners who got the team right, and I've seen those who have gotten the team wrong. The contrast in results is amazing. When there is a winning team, the attitude is positive, there is a can-do spirit in the air, communications are open and productive, and the business owner can leave with the assurance that the business will run well without them.

On the other hand, those who get it wrong tend to have a knot in their gut on the way to work in the morning. Tension is thick in the workplace. No one speaks, and, if they do, it is normally a complaint or criticism. Turnover is high. Those who join the team quickly realize it is not what they hoped for, and they search for a way to the exit. When the boss is gone, the work slows to a trickle. No one is happy. No one is having fun—especially not the business owner.

I sincerely hope the first example sounds more like you. If so, good for you! Use these next several weeks to fine-tune your team machine.

If, however, you can relate to the second example, you're in luck! Over these next weeks, you will learn how to turn that team into one that is a high-performing and well functioning unit.

A word of caution as we begin. Not everyone currently on your team may be able or willing to make the changes needed to become a winning team. Some cannot, and some will not, change. You must have the courage and conviction to either "change the person" or "change the person" if you know what I mean! Don't let a long-term employee, or a high-maintenance employee, or an aggressive employee detract you from your mission of building the best team possible—one that can run circles around your competition.

So this stage is simply a set up week. I'll briefly cover the Seven Keys to a Winning Team, and I will ask you to begin assessing yourself and your current team against these Seven Keys. Making changes in these areas will require as much change on your part as it will on those who work with you. After all, your team is simply following your lead. The question is are you leading them?

Key #1: Strong Leadership. You must demonstrate a conviction and determination to be a strong leader. I didn't say be nasty or mean; I said strong. There is a difference, and we will cover that in the next stage.

Key #2: Common Goal. It is critical for everyone on your team to understand the big goal. Having a clear and compelling goal is essential. More on this in Stage 33.

Key #3: Rules of the Game. Everyone wants and needs to know how the game is to be played, and where the boundaries have been set. No surprises. We'll talk about setting the boundaries in Stage 34.

Key #4: Action Plan. Everyone must have their own personal plan of action—what they are going to accomplish in the coming weeks, months, and years. If you are going to expect everyone to have a plan, then how important is it that there is a plan for the business? We'll discuss this in Stage 35.

Key #5: Risk Taking. Everyone makes mistakes; as the business owner, you must acknowledge the good efforts of your team, and help them to learn from good efforts that go badly. This can be a race changer if you navigate it well. We'll cover this in Stage 36.

Key #6: 100% Involvement. That's right, everyone must be involved! We're not asking folks to simply come in and do their tasks. We need everyone to have their head in the game if we're going to win. I'll share some great ideas in Stage 37.

Key #7: Know and Appreciate Your People. No matter how well you do Keys 1 through 6, if you don't get to know your folks, and show them that you care about them, you will not win their hearts. We are after their hearts—not just their brains or muscles.

There you have them, the Seven Keys to a Winning Team. Take some time this week to think about your business and how you engage with your team members. Jot down some notes or opportunities. I'll challenge you to think bigger and broader as we work through these next several stages.

STAGE 32
Demonstrating Strong Leadership

Welcome to Stage 32. You have entered the Team Region of the race where we will be covering the Seven Keys to a Winning Team. While you may be getting a bit tired and weary, I can assure you that now is not the time to take a break; instead, it is time to rely on your team to get you to the finish line. Developing a Winning Team is absolutely essential to your success if you ever hope to have the business working for you, rather than you working for the business!

The first key to creating a Winning Team is for you, the business owner, to demonstrate strong leadership. Sounds easy enough, doesn't it? Just be strong. Show your team that you are the leader.

So, you may be asking, "Ok, what's next?" Not so fast! I see more business owners who think they have "strong leadership," but are actually NOT leading; instead, they are just being a jerk or a grouch. Some mistake *strong* with *tough*. Others confuse *strength* with *short-tempered*. We should spend some time thinking through what it means to be a strong leader.

Here are a few characteristics you need to adopt if you are going to lead your team to victory:

Share a Compelling Vision: Strong leaders know where they are leading the team. They know the course so well that they can see it in their mind's eye. They know:

- Their goals
- Where the business will be a month or a year from now
- Who their future customers are
- What their future products can do
- How they will interface and link with their suppliers
- Who they will bring with them
- Who they will leave behind.

Strong leaders are excellent communicators. They paint the picture so that everyone on their team gets it. Their team members are highly motivated to achieve the crystal clear vision.

Surround Yourself with Talent: Strong leaders know they don't have all the answers. They are so comfortable in their own skin; they willingly bring talented advisors along side to help think through difficult challenges as they create their business of the future.

A great indicator of a strong leader is surrounding oneself with people who are even more capable than they are.

They are not threatened by others, but rather are energized by what they can accomplish working with those who have a different perspective, have more knowledge and experience, and those with wisdom.

Listen First: You can tell a strong leader by how much they talk versus how much they listen to others. The stronger the leader, the more they listen. When they do talk, they tend to ask questions rather than give direction or orders. Strong leaders know that they are the commander of the ship, but they like others to get engaged and think.

Set High Standards: Strong leaders set their expectations high, both for themselves and for the members of their team. Everyone around them knows they have their sights set high, and that they will do what it takes to achieve outstanding results. While setting the bar high is critical, it is also critical to hold people accountable to their expectations. There is no guesswork for a strong leader. Their team knows exactly what is expected, and they also know that there will be consequences for lack of effort.

Praise Others: Strong leaders are constantly on the look out for people doing things right. They are confident in their ability to get everyone in the business focused on doing the right thing by recognizing and rewarding those who step up and do more than is expected. I call this finding the "Moments of Truth."

Enjoy the Business: A sure sign of a strong leader is one who can find the time and opportunities to create enjoyment in the workplace. They are efficient at their work, and use their free time to boost other's fun factor. They are pleasant, friendly, engaging, and interested. They care more about their people than they do themselves—and it shows day in and day out. They never seem to have a bad day. They are confident that with the right people, the right attitude, and the right focus, they can solve any problem or climb any hill.

So there you have it; six specific behaviors that you can adopt this week to begin showing strong leadership. Your assignment for this week is to pick two behaviors that you think you need to improve upon, and focus on them.

Don't overwhelm yourself by trying to tackle all six behaviors of strong leaders at the same time. Be patient. Focus on two this week. You will begin to notice that your team will look up to you in a very different way as you demonstrate strong leadership.

Make a commitment now to work on them this week by listing the two behaviors here:

1. _____

2. _____

Stage 32 is all about making a change within yourself. It is not about anyone else on your team—it is about YOU! It is all about building your personal reputation and how your team will expect you to behave.

Step up to the challenge this week. Be honest with yourself about where you need to improve, and begin changing your behaviors this week.

You will like yourself more, your team will respect you more, and your business will benefit. This is the week for a win—win—win situation. Let's do it!

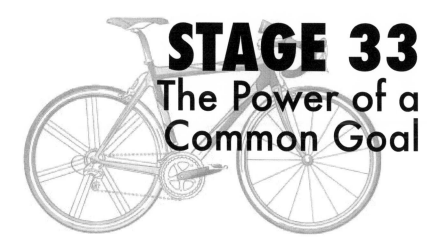

STAGE 33
The Power of a Common Goal

So how did you do on Stage 32? Did you take the time to reflect on your personal behaviors as a leader? Did you take the challenge seriously and focus on changing YOU first? I can assure you that, as the business owner, you set the tone and pace for progress for your organization. Don't seek to change others if you are not willing to change yourself!

So, with this renewed sense of your role as leader, it is time to move on to Stage 33 where the focus is creating a common goal for the team. This is a tricky or "technical" stage in the Tour de Profit. Unless you spend the time to give serious thought to this stage, you could easily cause your team to change their behaviors in a way that is not good for the long term success of the organization. Let me explain.

In an ideal world, your team would be motivated to help your business grow and succeed. They would not need or want external motivators to do the right thing. They would be so connected to, and aligned with, your vision and goals that they would want exactly what you do, as much as you do.

While this rarely occurs, you should strive to create a vision that is so compelling people want to work with you to make it happen. You should always be refining, sharing, and working on your vision to motivate your team intrinsically from the inside out.

I often see businesses with different goals for different departments, roles, or activities. Many times, these different goals are at odds with each other. For instance, sales managers love to create goals for their teams, and they will use the worn out idea that all good salespeople live for: recognition and reward. So they package a trip and bonus payment for hitting certain sales targets. Meanwhile, the rest of the organization work their tails off to support the sales team, but they get nothing except more work for their effort. The goal is designed for the sales team—not the entire organization. And because of that, there are often unintended, negative consequences for the business.

Common goals, on the other hand, can be uniting, uplifting, motivating, and inspirational to the entire team. To illustrate, let me share with you one of my experiences.

My company purchased a manufacturing company that was doing $30 million in annual sales. It had well over 200 employees located in two locations. While business was steady, the company was not growing. Profitability was well below our desired level.

After several weeks of assessing the situation, I decided that what was missing was a compelling common goal for everyone to rally around. I came to what I thought was a "clever" idea. I called a meeting of the entire team to share my observations, thoughts, and recommendations.

I pulled together a short list of matrixes that were critical for the business to grow and be more profitable. We set targets in each category that were reasonable and achievable. During the meeting, I shared the matrixes and the targets with the entire team along with our reasoning for each one. Then I unveiled my clever idea.

I told the entire team that the first month we achieved every target on our list, I would give my car to someone in the business! Now remember, this was a manufacturing business where the vast majority of our team members were factory workers living paycheck to paycheck. The offer peaked their interest.

Hands flew up all across the room. What kind of car is it? A four-year-old Jeep Grand Cherokee. What color? Hunter Green. Air Conditioning? Yes. Four-wheel drive? Yes. CD player? Yes. The questions went on and on. At that moment, everyone began envisioning that they could be driving in my car! That car could be theirs. All they had to do was work together, hit the targets, and then be lucky enough to be the 1 out of 200+ to be selected. Not bad odds for folks who were accustomed to playing the lotto!

As the weeks and months passed, the team began finding ways to work better together. Scrap and waste went down. Margin went up. Efficiency began improving in every area of the business. Every time I visited the factory, people would check out my car. Noses were pressed against the window. As I walked around, they would ask, "How's my car doing?" They were "owning" my car more and more every day.

A short five months later, we hit our targets—all of them! We arranged for a celebration, rented a large concert hall, invited everyone to bring their spouse and children, and catered a family-style dinner. I took my Jeep to a local auto detailer and asked him to make it look like new —which he did! Then we drove the Jeep into the building for the big event.

To decide who would drive away with my Jeep, we put everyone's names into a large drum. We picked out 20 names, and asked those individuals to come to the stage. They were the short list of potential winners.

To make things more interesting, I had stopped by the bank on the way to the celebration and picked up a large stack of $20 bills. I offered each of the potential winners to take $200 in cash before we drew down to 10. One guy quickly snatched up the $200 and took a seat.

We repeated the drill until my wife drew the winning name from the barrel. The lucky winner was a second-shift maintenance worker who had been with the company for over 20 years! We signed all the documents, gave him the keys, and took lots of pictures with him sitting in the Jeep with the biggest smile on his face!

The best part of the night was when I had the chance to say my closing remarks. I applauded the team, in front of their families, for their hard work and focus. After letting them know how proud I was of them, and how difficult it was going to be driving home with my wife who thought I had just lost my mind giving my vehicle away, I told them that I now knew they could do anything they put their mind to, and that I expected them to make the targets every month without question.

And that is just what they did from that point forward!

What an incredible night. All due to a compelling common goal that changed people's behaviors in a positive way!

So what is your common goal? What is your team focused on? Is it compelling? Is it motivating? Does it create a sense of teamwork that will lead to success?

I'm not suggesting you should give your car away. I'm not suggesting you have to come up with a cleaver idea. But, if you're serious about creating a Winning Team, you will spend time thinking about what would light their fire and bring the team together. Write down that goal here:

_____

_____

_____

Stage 33 is all about creating a common goal for your team. Take time this week to pull your thoughts together. I can assure you that, if you get it right, magic will happen!

STAGE 34
Establishing Rules of the Game

Welcome to Stage 34 of the Tour de Profit! You are in the region I call the Seven Keys to a Winning Team. This is where you define the kind of company you want to have by creating the right environment for your people to do their best work.

In Stage 33, we discussed why it was important to have a common goal for your team. I hope you took the time necessary to think it through and come to a compelling common goal. If you have not established your common goal yet, go back to the last stage, and get it done before you move ahead!

Don't get stuck trying to find the perfect common goal. Not everyone will warm up immediately to your thinking. Remember, it is your business. You decide what you want your business to become. Some will be energized by your common goal, and others may not. Those who are not energized may decide that your business is not right for them and leave. Wouldn't you rather they do that than stay around and make life miserable for everyone else?

Now, with your common goal in hand, you are ready to focus on the third key to creating a winning team: establishing your rules of the game. This is where you set the boundaries within which your team will work.

Before we get into the details, let me make sure you do not misinterpret the concept of "Rules of the Game."

Did you ever play Kick the Can or Capture the Flag when you were a kid. Yes, I know some of you are still playing those games today. How can I know this? Because I am. My kids are constantly asking to play, and I'm getting quite good at the strategy for Capture the Flag!

In those games, there are very few rules. But there are normally boundaries. Before the game starts, everyone agrees on where they can go, and where they can't go. As a parent, you may have some "off limits" areas that you just don't want the kids going into, or other areas that are off limits for safety reasons. In any case, boundaries are set.

Within those boundaries, once the game begins, everyone can do their own thing. Some chose to stay in one place; others run around a lot. In the end, the game is a blast, and everyone has fun.

This is not unlike what you should do in your business. Establish the Rules of the Game, set the boundaries, and then let your team enjoy their work!

Unfortunately, I find that many business owners play the game differently. They treat it more like having a dog with a shock collar and an invisible fence. When they hire a new team member, they put a shock collar on them, and don't tell them where the invisible fence is buried. Then, when something goes wrong or someone goes out of bounds, the owner hits the shock collar button to the surprise of the person wearing it.

The typical response is something like "What was that for?" or "I didn't know that was a big deal!" Rather than knowing the rules up front, the people on the team have to guess what they are.

Once they get the shock treatment, they will play the game safe. They will soon ask for permission before they do anything out of the norm. They become unmotivated and uninspired. The business owner tells everyone how hard it is to find good people these days. Sound familiar?

Establishing the rules of the game up front will help you avoid this scenario. How many rules, and what the rules include, are entirely up to you. Some may chose to have a long list of rules. Others prefer to have very few. Personally, I believe that if you want to get the most from your team, and want them to take ownership of their role in your business, you will set fewer rules.

A great book that I recommend you to read is *Drive* by Daniel H. Pink. The book outlines the three dimension of motivation that most business owners are missing. It is a great read, and has some eye-opening research results that will, no doubt, change your thinking about how to motivate your team.

I particularly like the idea of creating a ROWE: Results-Oriented Work Environment. Daniel describes this as moving beyond the cliché of "empowerment," and truly allowing your team members to do their work how and when they want to, with the only "rule" being that everyone will be accountable for their own results.

Now, I know this cannot work for many businesses. If you are in manufacturing, you can't have someone in the assembly area working from home, while others are waiting for them to do their part of the assembly. In retail, you have store hours and need staff to be available to service customers. But, in many businesses, and in many specific team roles, the results matter more than the traditional office work rules.

If you want to get the most creativity, engagement, and enthusiasm from your team, set as few rules as you can, and let them "own" their results!

Get the book. It is a must read for every business owner today.

So, your assignments for this week are these:

1. Read the book *Drive* by Daniel Pink.

2. Write down the essential Rules of the Game for your business.

3. Find the time to share the rules with your entire team.

Get out your calendar and schedule time, right now, to get these things done this week. Don't procrastinate. Your team will thank you, and your business will benefit from your attention to this important Key #3 to Creating a Winning Team.

STAGE 35
An Action Plan
for Everyone

How did you do with creating your rules of the game? Were you able to pick up the book *Drive*, by Daniel Pink as I suggested? What did you learn from your homework last week?

I am asking these questions because I know how significant an impact defining the rules of the game can have on your business' success. I believe it was Keith Cunningham who said there are only two sources of power for your business:

1. The people you hire and train

2. The culture you create

Defining your rules of the game will help define your culture, and, if done well, create true power for your business engine!

With your rules of the game in hand, we will move on to Stage 35 of the Tour de Profit. We are still in the region we call Seven Keys to a Winning Team region. This week, we will focus on Key #4: Action Plans.

It goes without saying that you can accomplish more when you have a plan to follow. That is true for each of us individually, and for our team of people working towards a common goal.

Think of an action plan as a syllabus for a course you are taking. The teacher would not think of going into the classroom day after day without a plan. In order to make sure all of the topics that will be on the test are covered, they map out the order in which the information will be covered, how long it should take, what the required reading will be, and what learnings should come from each lesson.

Why should you treat your business any differently? Do you have more invested in your business than you did in a class at school? I'll bet you have more invested in your business than it would cost to get a four-year degree from a select private college!

So, why would you not expect everyone on your team to be working from a written action plan? It only seems reasonable to expect that everyone who is working in your business will be able to articulate what they are working on, how it fits into the overall business plan, and what their time-line for completion is.

You have a written plan don't you? You could show it to anyone in your business at any time, right? If your banker asked to see your action plan, you could produce a copy for them, or could you?

First things first. If you do not have a plan as the business owner, then work on yours first! You MUST have an action plan. It MUST be written. It MUST be kept up to date. Preferably, it would be posted or available for anyone in the business to see. If you can't do that, how do you expect others on your team to link and align their plans to support yours?

As you are working on your action plans this week, there are some fundamental rules that should apply. These are intended to make sure your action plan will result in the most important element—ACTION!

There are many ways to put together action plans. I have a favorite that keeps me on target with my action plans; I SPAM each of my goals!

Why SPAM? You might think it is simply a processed meat product that comes in a can with a clever key to open it. But as they say in SPAM country, there are many, many uses for it. You can slice it and fry it as a breakfast meat. You can slice it, and make a sandwich for lunch. You can grind it, and make a spread for snacking. But, you can also use it to keep your action plan focused. SPAM your goals! Here's how:

S = Specific. Make sure each item in your action plan is specific. Write each item with enough detail so that anyone reading it would know and understand exactly what you intend to accomplish.

P = Personal. Assign each item in your action plan to a person—by name. Don't assign items to teams or groups. Assign action items to someone who can be responsible for the execution and completion of the action item.

A = Actionable. Write each item in your action plan in present tense with action-focused language. Make sure the focus is on doing something, not just considering, investigating, pondering, exploring, or discussing. Use words like: *complete, revise, transition, move, update, add, build,* or *create.* An action plan suggests you are taking action.

M = Measurable. Make sure every item in your action plan has a measurement tied to it. How will you determine if the action item has been done successfully? The measure may be a quantity. It may be a time frame. It may be an altitude or a temperature. Whatever fits the action item, make sure you are defining the outcome with a measurement.

Let's do it now. Choose one item from your action plan, and write it here:

Make it **Specific:** _____

_____

Make it **Personal**: Who is in charge of the item?

_____

_____

Write it in the present tense to make it **Actionable**:

_____

_____

How I will **Measure** it: _____

_____

I have found that when I SPAM my goals, my results are more certain. I have more clarity. My team knows what is expected of them. My business improves.

I believe in this concept to the point that I have a can of SPAM on my trophy case where everyone can see it. It is the constant reminder that everything we do must be done with these concepts in mind: Specific, Personal, Actionable, and Measurable.

What about you? Are you using SPAM in your business? Does everyone on your team have an action plan? Are they all in alignment and linked to the bigger goals of your business?

If not, this is the week for you to get them in place. Start with the most important person in your business—YOU! Share your action plan with your team, and ask them to create their own action plan to support yours.

You will be amazed at the power that comes from writing down your action plan, asking everyone to participate, and aligning them with the main goals of the business. It is like focusing a laser on a point; it creates an intensity that will burn through just about anything. This is your week to begin creating your laser-focused beam of light!

STAGE 36
Accelerate by Supporting Risk Taking

Welcome to Stage 36 of the Tour de Profit! We are in the heart of the Seven Keys to a Winning Team region. Over this seven-stage section of the race, we are diving deeper into the critical area of building the high-performance team to steer your business toward your long term goals.

We've covered the first four keys already, so you should be well on your way to creating an environment that will breed enthusiasm and productivity. As you recall, we covered Strong Leadership as the first key. Hopefully, you made some personal changes to improve in this area. Then, we covered the value of having a Common Goal, the second key. This alone can create positive change for your people. Next, with the third key, we reviewed the reasons why to establish rules of the game, so that your people can work without worrying about going out of bounds. Last week, the fourth key touched on the importance of having Action Plans across your business—starting with you, but reaching to everyone on your team.

This week, in Stage 34, we will focus our attention on the fifth key: Supporting Risk Taking. In this stage, we will explore the benefits of allowing your team members to stick their neck out without the risk of having it cut off.

Take a minute and think about how much latitude you give your team members. How much freedom do you give them to "do the right thing" or "take care of the customer" when the situation goes beyond the norm?

If you're like most business owners, you keep your folks on a pretty tight leash. How do I know? Well, think with me for a minute. How many times have you heard the phrase, "I'll have to get my manager to approve that," or "I can't authorize that without my supervisor's approval"?

Recently, I was checking into a hotel, and there was a discrepancy between the rate we had been quoted and the rate on the check-in sheet. When I brought it to the attention of the desk clerk, what do you think was her response?

Yep, you're right. She said, "Well, I'll have to clear that with my manager first, and she's not here right now." What do you think might have been my reaction to that? Was I impressed with the hotel? Did I think I was being treated like I was important?

Why do you think the desk clerk was not given the authority to make that kind of decision? Was it lack of trust, lack of training, concern over being taken advantage of? What are the reasons you don't give the authority to make exceptions to your team members?

Because the clerk did not have the power to address our concerns, we made the decision to have dinner somewhere else. As a result, the hotel lost an opportunity to capture the money we spent on appetizers, drinks, and dinner! Worse, because of our negative feelings, we are not going to recommend the hotel to others. We'll actually talk badly about the property.

So, for the sake of a minor misunderstanding, the hotel owner lost revenue, potential new business, repeat business, and good will.

Are your customers experiencing similar treatment from your team? Even if the individual incidences are small, they do add up.

I recall a situation that happened in my past business. We were late on the production of a critical unit for a big customer. To expedite the production, and reduce the shipping delay, we scheduled the unit to be built on the third shift.

When the shipping clerk realized that we were likely to miss the delivery date by putting the unit on the next delivery truck, he made a bold decision. He put the finished unit in his truck, and drove to the local airport where he kept his private single engine plane. Without asking anyone for permission, he flew the unit over 600 miles to the customer's location, arriving the morning that we had promised.

As you might imagine, when he returned there were mixed emotions. He had taken a huge risk, and gone way outside of our standard procedures. His decision cost the company a sizable amount of money in airplane fuel, but he met the commitment to the customer. Do you recognize and reward, or chastise and punish him? We chose a middle ground; we recognized his out-of-the-box thinking, and used it as a learning situation to avoid being late on future shipments.

If I asked your team members how you would react to them taking a risk and doing something outside the standard procedures, what would they say? Not sure? Why not ask them? Better yet, why not set the expectation that you want them to take the risk, when necessary for your customers? Let them know that you trust their judgment, and will always stand behind them—even if you think they did the wrong thing.

If done right, you can use these situations as a way to learn and improve your internal processes. Every time someone steps out and takes a risk, take the opportunity to recognize the effort, and make an improvement in your processes to avoid a similar issue in the future.

The ability to take risks can be liberating for your team. If they know you have their back when they take action for the benefit of your customers, they will become your strongest supporters and best sales people.

Try it this week. Find a time to have the discussion with your team, and make sure they know you support them, trust them, and expect them to resolve sticky issues themselves. You will reap big rewards when you not only have this meeting, but when you also follow through on your trust and support.

STAGE 37
Harnessing the Power of Everyone on the Team

Stage 37 takes us to the Key 6 to a Winning Team: 100% Involvement! It is difficult to decide which of the seven keys is most important, but this particular key can open the door to incredible results for your business.

The last five weeks have laid the groundwork for this critical stage. I hope you have been putting in place the fundamentals each week as we discuss how to create a business team that cannot be beat. If you think about it, the first five keys have positioned you to engage each and every person on your team.

So this week, we want to discuss how you can leverage all your efforts by getting everyone to be a part of your success.

I've seen many businesses where a few senior people act like they know it all, hold all the wisdom and knowledge, and make all the important decisions. Those with the "power" talk, act, and behave as if the others in the business don't get it, or don't have the brainpower to handle the difficult tasks and decisions.

When this happens, the employees blame those in power for every problem in the business. They have been trained to simply follow orders and "check their brain at the door"; therefore, the employees put forth little effort to improve the company.

I think I can safely say this is the number one reason why most people hate their jobs. They are treated like a worker—a thoughtless, mindless, clueless worker who is simply there to do what they are told, when they are told. They need heavy supervision. They are only there for a paycheck. If they are not watched, they will goof off. They don't give a hoot about producing a quality product. And they cannot be trusted.

When I see this, I immediately know where the problem is; not with the employees, but with the leaders.

Getting EVERYONE in the business engaged and involved in the success of the business is the only road to success.

But how do you get everyone involved? Here are a couple examples to give you some thought starters.

At my previous manufacturing company, we decided that the people on the assembly lines were the ones best suited to make improvements in time, cost, and quality of the production operations. Each week, we selected seven or eight different production workers to be part of a team to analyze their current assembly line processes, brainstorm improvements, test and measure their new ideas, and install the new processes on the assembly line. The team presented the new processes to the leadership team on Fridays during a regularly scheduled quality improvement celebration event.

Another example comes from a family-owned air-conditioning and heating company. The owners wanted to involve everyone on the team in the growth of their business. They created monthly contests where everyone, office staff and technicians alike, played in the contest. Each contest was very visual and cleverly "cute."

For instance, each month, walls at the shop were filled with little houses, little air conditioning units, little yard signs indicating the number of new units sold or new customers added or new service contracts signed. Instead of simply ending the day hot and sweaty, not concerned about increasing sales, the technicians were involved and engaged in the business of the company. They knew they were an important part of the team's success!

Write down some ideas of your own on how you can get your people involved in your business: _____

_____

_____

_____

_____

_____

_____

_____

Now, you have some work to do. Find an area of your business that could seriously use improvement; give the your team the assignment to come up with a recommendation for that area. Give them the latitude and resources they need, but only give them a short time frame to report back to you.

They will likely need access to some of your business data, or access to business records. Share it with them. Don't hold back. Treat them as if they were on your leadership team. Trust them completely. Go out of your personal comfort zone if necessary. Each and every one of them can help you build a stronger business if you involve them in the important decisions of the business.

Many on your team believe that they do not have the knowledge or ability to be more involved. They have been hearing this message for years, and they have worked in environments that did not engage their brains. It is easy to see how they might be short on self-confidence, but do not let them off the hook. Make them participate.

I can assure you that once you get them involved, show them you have confidence in them, support them, give them training and guidance, and expand their knowledge about the whole business, they will rise to levels you could never have imagined. How do I know this? I've watched it happen time and time again.

Have confidence, step out, get everyone involved and let them show you the way to building a better business!

STAGE 38
Know and Appreciate Everyone on your Team

We are onto Stage 38 in the Tour de Profit. As we head into the final third of the race, we are closing out the Keys to a Winning Team region. We've already covered six of the seven keys, so by now you should have put in place some strategies and practices that will make your team not only highly effective, but also highly engaged and passionate about growing your business.

But, your work in this critical region is not quite complete. This week we tackle what might be considered the most difficult stage in developing a winning team. Our topic this week is focused on you, the business owner or senior most leader. Your task this week is to genuinely get to know and appreciate each member of your team.

I am expecting that you are having one of two reactions: You might be saying to yourself, "No problem. I know all my people already, so this will be an easy week for me."

On the other hand, you might be saying, "You've got to be kidding. I've got 200 or more people on my team. There is no possible way that I can know and appreciate them all."

My response to both of these reactions is the same; you don't know what you don't know! Tune in, focus on this important topic, and you will realize that you have lots of room for improvement, no matter where you are starting from!

So let's dive in with this question, why is it so important that the business owner or senior leaders take the time to get to know and appreciate everyone on the team? Is this simply a feel-good activity, or is there a bigger benefit to the business?

I'll tell you that, without a doubt, this single strategy (if I may call it a strategy) can supercharge the first six keys to a winning team. Let me give you a couple of very real examples.

The CEO of a billion dollar manufacturing company made it a point to block a couple hours each week to do nothing else but walk through the office and the factory to speak with his team. He never went to the same places, and never had an agenda. He did, however, take the time to shake everyone's hand, ask what they were working on, and how things were going for them and their family. He did not know all of their names. He was not familiar with all of their families. But for that brief moment, the person he was talking with was the most important person in the world to him.

He spoke with top performers and below average performers alike. He spoke with long timers as well as new hires. His purpose was not to judge or critique. It was not to identify or solve problems. His purpose was to make his team know that he cared about them as a person. The result, as you might imagine, was low turnover, high performance, huge company loyalty, and a fun, friendly, functional workplace.

In contrast, another CEO of a consulting firm that had achieved significantly rapid growth took a different approach. He positioned himself as the most capable person in the business, and he made sure that everyone knew that if it were not for him, the business would be nothing. He would spend most of his time with his high performers, and wonder why others in the business just did not get it. Socializing was very important to this CEO, but his socialization often focused on other high-profile business leaders, knowledge experts, and celebrities. His engagement with team members was superficial.

While he was personally successful, the business was in a state of turmoil. Turnover was high. Frustration with the business systems was constant. A class system began to emerge between the "haves" and the "have-nots." Work was not fun or rewarding.

So which CEO do you resemble? I'd venture to guess that you are somewhere in the middle, not as extreme as either I have described. Which leads me to ask the question, why aren't you behaving like the first CEO?

What is stopping you from scheduling time to simply pay attention to the people who work on your team? Are you afraid that you might become too friendly with your team? I've heard that excuse more than a few times, and I think is it a line of bull. No one is going to take advantage of you because you care about their kids, or ask them about their sick mother, or are excited about their daughter's wedding.

Here's your challenge for the week. Find a way to surprise your team with your caring and kindness. Take a first step. Take a break with your technicians. Go to lunch with your accounting staff. Walk into your maintenance department and shake a few hands. It doesn't have to be radical, but it does have to be sincere.

Don't fake this one. If you're not serious about making your team members feel like you really know and appreciate them, just leave things as they are; you'll wish you hadn't tried in the first place.

I can say this with absolute confidence, your people will work ten times harder for you if they know you truly appreciate them. You'll see the difference in your business right away!

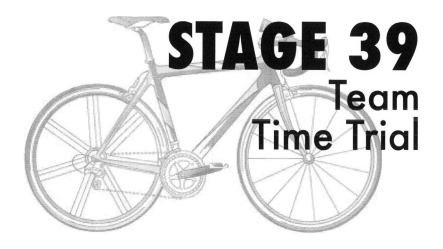

STAGE 39
Team
Time Trial

Congratulations on completing the Seven Keys to a Winning Team region! If you've done your work over these past seven weeks, you have positioned yourself and your business to be supported by a high-performance team who are as passionate as you are about your business. Frankly, it doesn't get any better than that!

This week we enter Stage 39 of the Tour de Profit. This week, your challenge is to demonstrate the new skills and capabilities you have learned about leading and motivating your team. After all, there is nothing quite as powerful as putting your new learning into action immediately.

So this week you will create a unique experience for your entire team. Here are some ground rules for your team activity. The activity should:

- Be the central theme for your week
- Be no less than half a normal workday

- Be off-site if possible, however an on-site activity can work
- Require interaction across functional areas of the business
- Build one another up
- Be fun
- Be novel

Think back over the Seven Keys to a Winning Team, and ask yourself, "Which ones do I most need improve upon?" Focus on that key by creating an activity that will support it. Be purposeful in the design of your activities.

To prime the pump, here are a few ideas to consider:

- Find an arcade or recreation center where your team can "play." These places often have staff members who specialize in team building activities.

- Host your team to a catered dinner combined with a memorable experience. You could take them out on a boat, go to a fun dance hall, or hold your event in an art gallery.

- Take your team to a baseball game, or other sporting event, where they can be recognized on the jumbo-tron.

- Reserve a park where you can have your senior leaders grill burgers and organize games.

The ideas can be endless. To get the best results, and to employ one of the keys, invite some on your team to get involved with the planning and organizing processes. You will immediately notice a higher level of excitement and enthusiasm.

When you introduce an out-of-the-norm experience, and show your team that they are important to you, their level of commitment and passion will immediately rise. The activity does not have to be fancy or expensive, but it does need to have your people at the center of the activity. This is not the time for you to boast or show off. This is the time to let the team see that you care about them, trust them, have confidence in them, value them, and appreciate them.

Take the opportunity to give out awards or personal recognition. Focus on the behaviors that you want the entire team to embrace. While it is certainly acceptable to recognize outstanding results, the more powerful approach is to recognize the behaviors you want to see in your business.

So, there you go. You've got your assignment for the week. Step out of the box this week. Let your people know you value them. Don't put it off. Do it this week.

Once you see the benefits from this assignment, you will certainly do it again. Good luck, and have fun! This is certain to be a great week!

STAGE 40
Think
Week

I hope that you took me seriously last week, and stepped out from your routine to do something special with your team. You've worked hard to build a team that allows you to beat your competition, so you should show them how much you appreciate them and value their contribution.

Now, we are off to Stage 40! And here's the good news, this is a rest week! Every now and then you need to get off the bike and recover. Rest your muscles. Take a break. Get some refreshment. We're well into this race, and it is high time for an off-week.

I know that for many of you it is hard to really unwind and enjoy life. So, for those of you who need to keep your engine running, I have a plan. I want you to spend the week as if you were Bill Gates! That's right. You can imagine that you are a billionaire who has everything, can go anywhere, and do anything. But instead of travelling, your going to spend your week in think time!

Bill is known to call this THINK WEEK. He steps away from his business, finds a quiet place to hang out, takes some reading materials, and spends his time thinking!

You would think that since we are all business owners we would dedicate some of our waking hours to just simply thinking, but most of us never slow down enough to do it. So that is your assignment for the week. Stop, sit, and think!

Go to your library, go to the bookstore, borrow a book from a friend, or download a book to your Ereader. It doesn't matter how. Just take time out of this week to put yourself into a setting that allows you to read and think.

I assure you that if you commit to finding time this week to genuinely think, you will be amazed by the clarity and focus that will come to you.

Try it; you'll like it! Enjoy the peaceful time this week!

STAGE 41
Benchmarking Your Competition

We are nearing the final stages of the Tour de Profit! This is not the time to slow down or give up. Instead, this is the time to begin your planning to win the race again next year. Remember, the stronger you get in your business, the more your competition will be using you as their benchmark.

So this week, in Stage 41, we are going to focus on benchmarking your competition. We know that your competition is watching your every move. They can see that something is different about you this year. You're more focused, more deliberate, and more strategic in your approach to the marketplace. They want to know what you are doing so they can quickly follow.

But, we do not intend to let them catch up! This is the week to gather information on your competition, and begin building your plan for next year's race so you can extend your lead, rather than give up ground.

Let's take a simple, methodical approach to bench-marking. We don't want to make this too complicated. We want our insights to be clear, so that we can easily translate them into action items for next year's plan.

To do this, I'll ask you to follow some simple steps this week. To make this more interesting, I suggest you enlist some of your team members in the process. The investigative work will be both interesting and thought provoking for them as well as for you.

First, write down the top five or six competitors in your marketplace. These will likely be businesses that are very similar to yours, but may also include business-es that provide alternative services or newly introduced products or services that you see as potential threats to your existing business. This will become your target list for benchmarking activities.

1. _____
2. _____
3. _____
4. _____
5. _____
6. _____

Second, dedicate 30-45 minutes to each competitor, and research their business online. Look at their website, and either make notes or print screen copies of their individual web pages. Collect ads or flyers to get an idea of the offers they are making. Read their blog posts. See what they are sharing with their customers and prospects. Go to their Facebook pages, Twitter accounts, and so on to see how they are positioning themselves in the marketplace. Determine if their key people have LinkedIn accounts, and read their pages. What are they reading, who are they connected with, what groups do they follow, and what credentials are they promoting. Build a file on each competitor with the major messages that they are sending to prospects.

Third, build a SWOT analysis sheet for each of your competitors. We did this exercise back in Stage 8. Remember, SWOT stands for Strengths, Weaknesses, Opportunities, and Threats. You want to outline what the strengths, weaknesses, opportunities and threats are for each of your competitors. The more data you collect, the better your SWOT analysis will be. Spend the time to get this down on paper so you can reference each SWOT analysis sheet as you begin to build your plan for next year.

Fourth, hold a review session with everyone involved in the data collection. Bring each of the SWOT analysis sheets to the meeting, and post them on a wall. Review them side-by-side, and look for patterns, trends, similarities, and different approaches. Capture your findings on a flipchart. What do you see when you look at your competition side by side? Who looks to be the competitor with the greatest momentum? Who is trying to change the way the game is being played?

Fifth, identify your SWOT as it compares with your major competitors. You will need to be brutally honest with yourself for this part of the exercise. Don't sugar coat what you're good at and where you need to improve. Do this well, and you will identify the critical areas of your business where you need to focus attention and get better.

Now is not the time to make decisions for next year. This stage is simply gathering and analyzing data. Next week, we will engage your current customers and get their inputs on your business. Once we have their inputs to consider, then we can begin building a plan. Be patient. Don't try to make a quick decision. We want to have multiple views to consider before we build our plan.

Do this well, and your plan will be solid for next year's race!

STAGE 42
Getting Customer Feedback

In last week's stage, we focused on your main competition. You did the research, collected intelligence on their product and service offerings, reviewed their websites, collected their flyers, and spent the time building a SWOT analysis for each of your primary competitors. Good for you! This insight will be valuable as you begin to build your plan for next year's race.

Now we turn our focus to YOUR business. And who better to give you feedback on how well you are delivering on the promises you make than your existing customers?

Welcome to Stage 42. Your current customers hold the key to some of the most valuable competitive information you could ever gather.

Think about it; your current customers have already made a choice about your competition. They are voting with their pocketbooks, which is the most powerful indicator of market preferences. Your customers have done some comparative shopping, and they have determined that your offer is the most compelling, your product is superior, your pricing is acceptable, and your delivery meets their needs.

Would you agree?

Not so fast! How can you be sure? What if they are on the verge of dropping you? How would you know? What if their last visit was just that—their last visit?

Isn't it important to know what they are feeling about you and your business? How often do we make an assumption that everything is going well without asking our customers about their feelings and perspective?

This is the week to change all that. This week, your assignment is to do something that many of your competitors rarely do—talk with your customers, and ask them directly what they think about doing business with you.

Before we compile our data and insights into a plan, we must have this critical piece of intelligence. The intelligence we gain from our customers is what is most critical to our future success. It is like the blood that flows through our veins. It is important to have good blood.

As we have done several times before, I want to give you a step-by-step process to follow this week. There is no need to make this complicated. We'll break down your activities into easy, logical steps that will give you the outcome you need and want—the honest truth from our current customers. Ready? Here we go:

Step 1: Gather a list of all the customers that have purchased from you over the past six months. We want those who are current customers, not those who did business with you a couple of years ago. The more current the better.

Step 2: Sort the list by frequency of purchase and total purchase volume. We want to know which customers do business with you on a very regular basis. Their purchases may be small in relative size, but if they are regular, repeat customers. That makes them very valuable to you over the long run. We also want to know who does a large volume of sales with you. These may be infrequent customers, but, when they buy, they buy big. These too are critical to your long-term success.

Step 3: Start at the top of each list and identify a manageable number of customers who you could have a one-to-one discussion with over this next week. If you have others on your team who can assist with this activity, give them a manageable list as well. The more the better, but it is better to have a meaningful discussion with a few, rather than a brief and surface level discussion with many.

Step 4: Build a list of five or six key questions that you would like to ask each customer. These would be open-ended questions—they cannot be answered with a simple yes or no, or a single word. You want these questions to be relevant, but also thought provoking. An example might be, "What is the feeling you get when you do business with us?" That question may cause them to wrinkle their forehead and pause for a minute, but the response will be very revealing. Write your questions here:

1. _____
   _____

2. _____
   _____

3. _____
   _____

4. _____
   _____

5. _____
   _____

6. _____
   _____

Now come up with four or five other questions that get at the heart of your product, service, accessibility, ease of doing business, follow through, etc. Focus on those areas of your business that matter most, and those that may be strategic for you.

1. _____
   _____

2. _____
   _____

3. _____
   _____

4. _____
   _____

5. _____
   _____

Step 5: For every primary question you identify, come up with a secondary question that digs deeper into their answer. These will likely be "why" questions. For example, "Why does that matter so much to you?" or, "Why would that make a difference in who you do business with?" The goal is to get your customer to reveal more of their underlying reasons for choosing you over your competition.

Step 6: Make copies of your questions so that you have one set of questions for every customer you plan to visit with. Don't try to "wing it." Let them know that you are gathering data to make strategic decisions for your business. They will be honored to know you included them in your process.

Step 7: Give yourself and your team members a goal of completing all discussions by a certain day and time. Don't let this process linger. Set the expectation that this is urgent and important. Allow yourself and your team to schedule blocks of time to either visit your customers in person, or connect with them by phone. Make this a live interaction. No e-mail. No Survey Monkey. No questionnaire in the mail. Talk with your customers either on the phone or in person. They will appreciate you reaching out and making the connection.

Step 8: Gather the data and compile the results. I know what you are thinking, these will be all verbal responses; no numbers to average. How does that help? This is not an effort to be scientific. It is about making a "touch," and building a deeper relationship with your best customers.

You want to grow your business; spend time talking with your customers!

There you have it. Eight simple steps. Nothing fancy. Once you put this information and insight with your competitive SWOT intelligence, you are ready to make some decisions, and build a plan for future success.

Well done! Your customers are impressed that you care, and you know more clearly what you need to do to gain more great customers. What could be better than that?

STAGE 43
Building Next Year's Race Plan

Congratulations on your efforts over these past two stages. You have gathered intelligence on your competition, and reached out to your best customers to get their feedback on your opportunities for improvement. While it is difficult to determine absolute importance, these efforts on your part may be the most significant and important pieces of work you have done during this Tour de Profit.

The hard work has positioned you to begin putting together your plan for next year's Tour de Profit. Armed with the insights from your toughest competitors, and from your best customers, you can build a plan that will take your business to the next level. To build this plan, you need a simple, yet comprehensive, model to follow. That is your assignment for this week in Stage 43.

I want to introduce you to a nine-category model that covers the critical areas of your business that you must include in your game plan for next year. These nine categories will help you structure your business plan and focus your strategic actions on the areas that matter most. Here is a brief overview of each of these nine categories, and the kinds of questions you need to address in each category:

Compelling Vision: How clear is your long-term vision? Does each member of your team know, understand, and feel energized by your vision? What is needed to make it clearer, more compelling, and more real to those who will help you achieve your compelling vision?

Lead Generation: What are your best strategies to get more prospective customers to know your business exists? How effective are the strategies you are currently using? What can you do to improve your cost per lead? Do you have a robust CRM system in place?

Lead Conversion: Is your current sales process well defined and used by everyone on your team? Are you tracking the results of each step of your sales process? Are you asking the right kinds of questions of your prospects? Do they want to do business with you?

Delighting Customers: How do you know what your customers really think about your products and services? Are you gathering customer feedback on a regular basis? What would you do differently to improve your customer experience?

Generating Repeat Business: Do you know your average sales ticket? Do you know your average frequency of purchase? What strategies are you using to get your current customers to buy from you more often?

Building Leverage Through Processes: How many of your critical processes are well documented with checklists posted in the work area? What opportunities do you have to standardize routine processes? Where can you gain efficiency, and reduce costs, by eliminating unnecessary actions or mistakes.

Building a High-Performance Team: Does everyone on your team have a personal development plan? How do you encourage risk taking in your business? Have you communicated your expectations in terms of your non-negotiables?

Creating a Succession Plan: Have you defined your ideal transition scenario for your business? What have you done to prepare your key leaders to potentially become general managers? Have you outlined the skills, behaviors, and knowledge required of your successor?

Giving Back to the Community: What are you currently doing to be a good steward and contributor in the community? Have you defined a charity or service organization that you and your business can adopt? Are you seen in the community as a business that gives generously to those in need?

With your competitive assessment and your customer feedback in hand, and a planning model that you can follow, you can now begin building your plan. First set your goal of what you want to accomplish over the next year.

Goal: _____

_____

Next, identify the top two or three specific actions that need to be addressed to achieve your goal.

1. _____
   _____

2. _____
   _____

3. _____
   _____

Lastly, turn these specific actions into SMART goals – goals that are Specific, Measurable, Achievable, Responsible (assigned to someone specific), and Time bound.

Action:

Specific: _____

Measurable: _____

Achievable: _____

Responsible: _____

Time: _____

Action:

Specific: _____

Measurable: _____

Achievable: _____

Responsible: _____

Time: _____

Action:

Specific: _____

Measurable: _____

Achievable: _____

Responsible: _____

Time: _____

Focus your efforts this week and you will have a solid foundation for your race plan next year.

STAGE 44
Defining Your Key Performance Indicators

Stage 44 of the Tour de Profit is designed to take your race plan (otherwise known as your business plan) from a collection of great ideas and potential business-building strategies, and convert it into a meaningful set of measures and metrics that you can use to track your progress and quantify your results. This is where you define your Key Performance Indicators (KPI).

Before we start, let's get clear on what KPIs are and what KPIs are not. KPIs are not the same as your monthly financial measures. They are *not* revenues, profit, margins, or numbers of customers. These are backward-looking metrics because they show you what happened in the past. Still, they are important numbers to know in your business because they are the results of the activities you are doing, and they are the outcomes from the decisions you made, and the activities you engaged in.

Many business owners like to use what happened in the past as predictors of what will happen in the future. In some cases that makes sense, but what we want to do is identify and build a set of metrics that are more current, and that generate outcomes such as more customers, revenues, profits, and greater margins.

To be sure we are clear on this point, here are a few examples of KPIs that a business should track and measure:

- Number of leads generated
- Number of appointments held with prospects
- Number of proposals made
- Average register sale
- Average frequency of purchase

The list can go on and on, but what you see from this list are early indicators for acquiring a new client, increasing revenues, etc. These early indicators are what you will want to measure to help predict what your revenue and profit growth will be throughout the coming year.

You want to measure your efforts on a weekly basis, not on a monthly or quarterly basis. This will allow you many more opportunities to review your activities, make adjustments, and make improvements.

With this basic understanding, your assignment this week is to design and build your KPIs for next year's race. Again, let's take a simple approach to this exercise.

Go back and review the work you did in the last stage where you considered the nine critical areas of your business. In each of the nine critical areas, ask yourself, "What would be the best measure of activity or results? What would demonstrate that you are making progress?" Focus on the activities that you do every week. Don't make it a complicated calculation. Keep it simple.

If the critical area is lead generation, then consider new leads generated, or number of networking groups attended, or number of responses to an advertisement.

If the critical area is delighting customers, then consider the average score on satisfaction surveys received, or average wait time for your services, or average deliver time of an order. These are the kind of leading indicators that you will want to track and measure to give you a sense of whether you are improving or falling backward.

Once you have a list of potential KPIs that cover all nine critical areas, you can prioritize, and select the top five or six that will be most important for your business growth this next year.

KPI 1: _____

KPI 2: _____

KPI 3: _____

KPI 4: _____

KPI 5: _____

KPI 6: _____

These KPI's will form the beginning of your metrics dashboard. Find someone on your team with the skills and interest to create graphs and charts from raw data. Give them the assignment to put each key metric on a graph so you can begin to see the weekly trends.

Focus on these KPIs first. Communicate them to your team, and instruct everyone on how and when the data will be collected, who will be responsible for updating the KPI graphs, where they will be posted, and how you plan to review them regularly. Be specific in your assignments, and engage your team in bringing your KPIs to life.

This activity will turn your strategic planning into tangible, measurable activities that everyone can see and use. Nothing changes behaviors faster than performance metrics posted so everyone can be held accountable!

Good luck defining your KPI's this week. You will be glad you put in the effort to make this a priority.

SYNERGY
REGION

STAGE 45
Creating Synergy

Welcome to Stage 45 of the Tour de Profit! With only eight stages left the race, it is time to begin putting all the pieces together.

This week, Stage 45, we enter the Synergy Region of the race. This is the region where we focus on leadership, both for you personally and for your team. The goal for this region is to prepare your business to be led by those around you. This is the point in the race where you begin to lay the groundwork for building leaders, delegating the more critical tasks, and positioning yourself to move away from the day-to-day details of your business.

Over the next several weeks, we will be covering the five critical areas necessary to create synergy within your business. These include creating your Personal Development Plan, building a Team Developmental Plan, introducing

Performance Assessments into your business, developing your General Managers, and building a Succession Plan.

These five areas are critically important to any business owner who hopes to one day have a team of people who can run the business on a day-to-day basis, freeing up the business owner to focus on the next great opportunity. Rather than wait for opportunities to present themselves, you will be able to prepare yourself and your team for the opportunities, even though you may not know exactly what they are right now.

Leadership requires study. Leadership requires planning. Those who look to you for leadership are watching to see what you find important. That is why our first stage in the Synergy region will focus on the most important team member—you.

As you prepare yourself for the Synergy region, this is the week to begin thinking about what you want to be included in your own personal development plan. We'll go into detail on it next week, but this is a great time to think about what you hope to gain from the Synergy region.

You've been riding a good race. You have positioned your business well. You are seeing the benefits of your hard work and determination to build a great company. Now is the time to begin thinking about leadership. This is about building a sustainable enterprise—one that will work without you just as well as if you were still at the controls. Creating synergy within your team, and focusing on developing yourself and your people, will put you in a great position to out-race your competition.

Take time this week to write down what you believe your business could be like if others in your business were equipped and prepared to take the leadership roles. What would it free you to do if you had a team who could handle the day-to-day operations? What would you focus on next to take your business to the next level? _____

_____

_____

_____

_____

_____

_____

_____

_____

_____

_____

Now, get yourself prepared this week for the stages ahead. They could be game changing for your team, your business, and your future.

STAGE 46
Creating Your Personal Development Plan

Exceptional leaders are constantly working harder on themselves than they are on their business! The success of any business is limited only by the thinking, knowledge, and growth of the senior-most leaders.

Welcome to Stage 46 of the Tour de Profit. This week, we focus our effort on the first critical step to build Synergy in your business: creating YOUR Personal Development Plan. We are going to discuss not only why it is important to have your own development plan, but also what should be part of your plan and how to get started. Ready? Let's get on the road!

First, let's assess where you are right now. If you have a personal development plan, pull it out. I would suspect that 95 out of 100 of readers of this book do not have one. If you do, let me say congratulations! Simply having your thoughts in writing is a great step in the right direction.

I believe that the reason most business owners do not have a personal development plan is that they think it is too much work and too hard to maintain. I want to show you that it can be put together and maintained easily if you follow some very simple steps.

First, take a few minutes and write down the nine or ten things that you must be excellent at in order for your business to be successful. If you are a solopreneur, your list may include specific technical skills related to your product or service. If you have a small team of people, your list may include some technical skills, but also some people-related skills (delegating, accountability, etc.). If you have a larger business with direct reports who manage others on your team, your list should include more strategic items, some team-oriented skills, and perhaps some systems-building capabilities.

It is important to first build the list of things that matter most to you and your business. Don't get distracted by what others tell you is most important. Focus on where your business is today, where you want it to be in two to three years, and what the gaps are that you need to cover to get there. These gaps will help you identify the critical development areas that either you or one of your key people must have on their development plan. For now, focus on those that you believe you must master yourself. Write them here:

1. _____

2. _____

3. _____

4. _____

5. _____

6. _____

7. _____

8. _____

9. _____

10. _____

Now, take a single sheet of paper and divide it into four quadrants. We'll let each quadrant represent one quarter of the year: 1Q, 2Q, 3Q and 4Q. This will help you visualize your next year, so you can prioritize your activities.

Next, review your list of required skills and place them into one of the four quadrants based on the urgency with which you believe they must be in place. Limit each quadrant to only two or three specific skill areas. Adding more would not be productive or achievable. It is better to work with a shorter list of skills, and get really good at them, rather than do a fly-by on several skills.

Now that you have your critical skill development areas positioned across the four quarters of the year, add into each quadrant two additional and recurring items: Think Time and Business Planning. If you include these into your personal development plan, you will be more likely to schedule time to do them, and your team will see that you consider them important.

So there you are. In four simple steps, you have the essence of a simple, usable developmental plan. It does not need to be fancy. There is no special form required. The content matters far more than the look and feel of the plan. With this essential framework in place, you can begin researching what the best courses, tools, seminars, groups, etc. to gain the new skills you need.

Spend a few minutes each month to schedule the necessary events and activities on your calendar. Always be looking two to three months ahead, so you have enough open time to commit to your plan. Get your quarterly business planning events on your calendar. Block time to think each quarter.

Make a commitment to yourself and your team to follow through on your plan. If you want them to take personal development seriously, you need to lead by example. Take this week to set a great example. Have your plan complete before the week is out. Share your plan with your team. It will have a positive impact on them and on your business.

STAGE 47
Using Personal Development to Fuel your Growth

Congratulations for taking the time to create your own Personal Development Plan! I trust you have shared it with your team, so they understand what you believe is important, and that you are serious about getting better yourself.

With your plan in hand, it is time to move ahead to Stage 47 of the Tour de Profit. We are in the Creating Synergy region. In these critical stages of the race, you are focused on preparing your business for growth by preparing yourself and your team to handle bigger, more strategic issues within your business.

This week's stage is focused on using personal development to fuel your growth. You want to tap into the limitless potential of your team members, and get them fully engaged in growing your business. To do this, we are going to take a position that everyone in your business has the ability to do more, and has the desire to do more. The only thing lacking is the motivation to step it up.

Here's a news flash—most people who are working for someone else are doing far more complicated, technically challenging, and higher impact work OUTSIDE of their paid job! Think about how many people willingly and enthusiastically volunteer their time to church, social clubs, schools, hobbies, and sports. In many cases, they pour themselves into their volunteer efforts, and take on far more difficult assignments.

Why is that? I have a theory; they receive more thanks and appreciation, more recognition and reward, more personal gratification from their volunteer efforts than they do from their boss!

I don't want to get too deep into all the reasons why they might feel this way. I'll remind you to go back and review the earlier stages where we covered building a high performance team. Many of the answers lie there. But for this week, let's stay focused on one important aspect—making your team members feel like they are important to your business.

How we do this is by helping them build their own Personal Developmental Plan. By simply talking about it, giving them some guidance and direction, and helping them put their plan together, you will impress upon them their future role in your business. When they see themselves as an important part of the team, their commitment and drive will increase.

Let me give you a simple way to get started. Remember how we created your plan? You listed the top nine or ten things you need to be excellent at in order for your business to be successful. I want you to change this to a list of areas that your business needs to improve upon in the next two or three years. List them here:

1. _____
2. _____
3. _____
4. _____
5. _____
6. _____
7. _____
8. _____
9. _____
10. _____

Now give this list to each member of your team with an assignment. Have them come back to you with their thoughts on the following:

1. Which of these areas do they think they could help with the most?

2. What could they do to get better in this area?

3. What skills do they need to gain or improve upon?

4. What books could they read to understand this area better?

5. Who would they like to be their accountability partner to help them make improvements in this area?

Next, take the same approach that you used last week to create four quadrants on a page. Have them put their thoughts and ideas into each of the four quadrants representing the four quarters of the year. Make sure that each quarter includes a specific skill-improvement focus and a specific book to read.

This plan does not need to be complicated or fancy. Simply get them to take the time to build a plan of action. Assign them an accountability partner—preferably one of their own choosing—and then get started! You will refine and improve your system as you go. In the meantime, your team members will begin making improvements to the planning process!

Finally, schedule time in the future to review their plans. Don't miss this step. They will put more effort into their personal development if you ask them about it, review their progress, and give them encouragement along the way.

There you go. Get these things done this week, and your team will soon be as motivated as you are to make personal improvements!

STAGE 48
Changing Behavior through Performance Assessments

Have you ever wondered whether performance assessments really work? Most of us have been involved with performance reviews. We remember our experience as being impersonal, subjective, and punitive. The administration of these processes was largely complicated, bureaucratic, and largely ineffective.

So I can imagine as you enter Stage 48 of the Tour de Profit that you're not excited about the idea of introducing performance assessments into your business. But before you decide this is a bad idea for your business, I'd like to introduce a few thoughts on how you can use performance assessments to positively change behavior within your business.

We are right in the middle of the Creating Synergy region. This is where you're trying to gain advantage over your competition by improving your personal leadership skills, growing new leaders, and positioning your business for rapid growth. As you know, growth does not occur without new learnings and constructive feedback.

In this week's stage, I will introduce you to a structured approach for providing constructive feedback.

Many business owners who give performance reviews use a haphazard approach. They scratch out a few minutes from their busy schedule to meet with their employees. The meeting is not pre-planned, the discussion is not thought through in advance, and the employee is often surprised by what they hear. The boss leaves the meeting glad it is finally over, and dreads the thought of doing it again next year!

This approach does not build morale or create positive change in the business.

Let me touch briefly on the three critical elements of a successful performance assessment. First, the process must evaluate what work gets done against established standards. Second, the process must evaluate how work gets done against established norms. And third, the process must allow for self-evaluation in addition to supervisor and/or peer review.

Your assignment this week is to document the fundamentals of your Performance Assessment process. We'll make this easy by having you follow a simple recipe or formula:

Step 1: Establish your work standards to measure WHAT the individual has accomplished. This can be as easy as defining three different levels of work performance: Superior, Expected, and Below Expectations. (You can add other levels if you need more degrees of separation).

Step 2: Establish your behavior standards to measure HOW work gets accomplished. Again, this can be as easy as defining three different levels of teamwork and behaviors: Superior, Expected, and Below Expectations.

Step 3: Write a one or two sentence description of each level of performance for both the WHAT (Step 1) and the HOW (Step 2).

Step 4: Share your standards and descriptions with everyone on your team. They must know what standards they are being measured against.

Step 5: Determine how frequently you will provide this feedback to your team members. At a minimum, it should be yearly, but ideally, it would be every six months.

Step 6: Schedule 30 to 45 minutes with each of your team members to discuss their performance. Allow them to give themselves a self-assessment based on your criteria and descriptions. Use this opportunity to discuss what they need to focus on over the next six months.

You do not need to make it any more complicated than this. It does require some pre-work and planning. The more thought you put into the criteria and descriptions the better. Don't get wrapped up in documents and forms, structure and formality. Once you get started, you can always add more structure and documentation. It's better to get started this week than to wait until everything is perfect.

In the end, people simply like to know how they are doing, and how they can get better. Give them the best chance to be successful by creating a performance assessment process you will follow on a regular basis.

STAGE 49
Developing
General Managers

How do you position yourself to move away from the day-to-day details of your business? This may be one of the biggest single issues facing business owners. It is not uncommon to get trapped in the details of a business to the point where you cannot find the time or energy to groom your replacement.

Welcome to Stage 49 of the Tour de Profit. We are in the Synergy region where we are focused on building leaders. This particular stage is centered on developing your senior-most leader: the General Manager. You can add whatever title makes sense for your industry, but essentially, this individual is responsible for the overall performance of your business, from top to bottom.

Let me ask you, how comfortable are you turning over your business to someone else? How confident are you that they will make decisions you will agree with and that will be good for the long term success of your business? How knowledgeable is he or she about the needs of your most important clients? These are critical questions that must be addressed in order to put someone into this critical position.

It is easy to see this is not a simple decision. It requires a significant amount of thought and preparation. In fact, in some businesses, it may take months or even years to prepare someone for this assignment.

Since this is not a quick-response decision, doesn't it make sense to approach it with a thoughtful plan? Let me give you a few thoughts for forming your plan.

It is critical that you create a detailed job description for the General Manager position. There are generic descriptions available online at tourdeprofit.com in the Resources area that will give you some ideas and suggestions. I'd suggest you start there, and make changes based on the specific activities and areas of focus for your company. It is often far easier to make changes to an existing document than it is to create one from scratch. If you have one from a prior business or from a colleague, "steal" the framework and edit with your specific content.

In the end, this document should be very descriptive about the tasks, responsibilities, structure, and success measurements for the position.

I would strongly recommend that you "step it up a notch" from where you are currently managing the business. Stretch the assignment to take on more responsibility, add more discipline, and set higher standards than you do for yourself. While many business owners are their own toughest critics, it never hurts to set the bar higher for a new General Manager, particularly since you are going to be in the background, ready to help them succeed.

Once you have the job description in hand, make a list of the critical skills that a General Manager must have to be successful in your business. These may include technical training, systems or software training, leadership training, or even selling skills. No matter what they are, document them. This may become a checklist for a prospective GM, or it may become a critical part of a development plan for your new General Manager candidate.

With this key skills list, you can begin assessing your current team members for future potential, or use it as a standard for hiring a prospective general manager.

In many cases, it takes months, if not years, to prepare someone for this critical position. So even if you are not planning to step away from your business for some time, it is best to begin the preparation. Not only will you be prepared, but your team will also know you are thinking about the long-term success of the business. Don't be afraid to let your team members know your plans, so they can prepare themselves for the eventual change in leadership.

Take this assignment seriously. You will never make a more important hiring decision. The individual who will replace you in the business must be a great fit for the position, both today and in the future. Spend time in planning and preparation to improve the likelihood of making a smooth, successful transition.

RESULTS
REGION

STAGE 50
Building a Succession Plan

When was the last time you put some serious thought into what you would do after you sold or transferred your business to someone else? Seriously? I know we all have those moments when we are so frustrated that we say, "Just take this business away from me. I'm done with it!"

But that is not what I'm talking about. I'm talking about the serious, deliberate discussion with your inner circle of advisors about the success of your business. Why aren't you having this discussion? Is it too soon to be talking about a succession plan? Are there too many issues that need to be resolved in the business? Really?

Welcome to Stage 50 in the Tour de Profit. We are now in the Results Region. This is the final leg to victory.

This week's stage is focused on building a Succession Plan for your business. That's right, we're going to discuss

219

how you prepare to make an orderly transition to a new owner of your business. Having that discussion well before the event will result in a more thoughtful plan, one that is not tainted by the emotions that are certain to rise up as the time for transition nears.

Why is this such an important topic? Because every business owner will eventually go through a transition of ownership. Whether it is a transition to a family member, a sale to an existing employee group, a sale to an external buyer, or one of the three Ds of business: disability, divorce, or death. Every business will go through a transition from one owner to another.

Fast-forward in time, and imagine yourself at the stage of your life and the life of your business where you have decided it is time to sell. Take out a note-pad, and write down the things that are most important to you about how that transition will occur. This can be a list of concerns or a narrative of the situation, emotions, people involved, and desired outcomes. Put it in language and a format that works for you.

Then answer these kinds of questions: Who are the specific people you want involved in the process? How will you share the news with your key people? What are the specific outcomes that you want to occur? What are you doing following the event? Where are you going? Who are you going with? What is the predominant feeling that you and your spouse have as a result? Most importantly, get your thoughts down on paper.

If this is the first time you have given succession much thought, you may need to begin the list and come back to it from time to time to add additional thoughts. Whether you do this in ten minutes or ten days, it is important to get your thoughts together before you begin having discussions with others. Not that you should ignore their wise counsel, but I find it beneficial to always do your own thinking first, making adjustments as necessary.

Once you have a complete picture of your desired transition, schedule time to visit with your close circle of advisors. You can either visit with them one by one, or you can call them all together and share your thoughts. I believe it is best to gather those you trust together, so they can hear your ideas and desires, ask questions, and be prepared as a team to help.

My experience is that most business owners do not take advantage of the knowledge, experience, and wisdom of their close advisors. Rather than calling a small group together to think through this important transition, many will simply try to execute a transition on their own, or with the help of a previously unknown outside third party broker. What a missed opportunity!

Lean on those you know, trust, and respect. They will help you think through many aspects of a succession plan that would otherwise be missed. Take this opportunity to gather additional notes, list critical issues to address, and note potential mine fields.

With these insights and valuable advice, you are much better equipped to make the right decisions, at the right time, to achieve your desired outcome.

Building a succession plan is as much about putting your thoughts on paper as it is about deciding who should replace you as leader of the business. Most corporate organizations think of succession plans as simply replacing one person for another. But for business owners, succession is far more significant, and far more complicated. That is why you should schedule the time to create this plan now. You can always revisit the plan and make adjustments as you get closer to the actual decision date.

Take the time this week to build your plan. It will add clarity to the critical issues in your business, and at the same time give you peace of mind that you are thinking ahead and making thoughtful decisions.

STAGE 51
Recognizing Your Best Customers

As we near the end of the Tour de Profit, it is appropriate to take time to recognize those who have helped you achieve your success. I know that the first group who come to mind is your team, those who have worked hard in your business all year long delivering on the promise you made to your customers. There is no doubt that these folks deserve your thanks and attention.

But I want you to spend this week recognizing an even more important group—your customers! Think about it; you would not even have team members if you did not have customers! There would be no need for documents, processes, procedures, or systems if you did not have good customers. Your customers are without a doubt the most important people to your business's success.

So, here's your question for this week: What are you doing to make sure your customers know how important they are to you? How will you recognize their value to you and your business? How will they know, beyond a shadow of a doubt, that you value them, respect them, admire them, and appreciate them?

Anything you do to show appreciation to your customers is worth doing with a personal touch! If you are going to send a note, make it a personal note. If you are going to send a card, make it a personal card. If you are sending a gift, make it something that relates to that particular client.

I used to receive a fruit basket every Christmas holiday from one of my suppliers. When the box arrived, I knew who had sent it. Unfortunately, without exception, when I opened the box I'd find a standard packing list and an order form. There was no note other than the standard, "Thanks for your business" on a small card that doubled as a marketing piece.

Was I impressed? No. Did I like the fruit? Sure. Did it make me appreciate the sender more? Not really. Did it make me do more business with them? Nope.

Why not be different? Why not stand out from the crowd? Why not do something that really matters—something that gets the kind of response you hope for?

Need ideas? Great! Here is your assignment. Ask three or four of your colleagues what they are doing to recognize their best customers. Then steal the best ideas! Yes, it is ok to steal ideas—it is called benchmarking. Business owners do it all the time.

If you don't hear any good ideas, collaborate with a colleague, and have them ask a few of *your* customers what would make them feel special. You can do the same for your colleague.

Here's the best part, even if you don't come up with any new, creative ideas, you will get some good customer feedback that will be valuable to your business. And you get it for free!

But, just so you don't go empty handed, here are a few ideas to consider:

- Recognize your best customers on your website with a story of what makes them special.

- If your business is B2B, include links to your customers' websites in your newsletter with a personal note of thanks and a referral.

- Invite your best customers to a happy hour or dinner where they can meet others who have similar interests.

- Give out customer awards, even if you have to make them up!

- Send them something unique and specialized.

- Send them tickets to a special event for their family with a personal note attached.

If you're thinking, "These are good ideas, but each of them will cost a lot of money," then you need to re-set your thinking. Take a minute to remind yourself of the lifetime value of a good customer. If a good customer stays with you two or three years, and they do multiple transactions with you, the cost of a special gift or personal invitation is comparatively small.

Take this week to recognize your best customers. Over the long term, it is one of the best ways to grow your business.

STAGE 52
Spending Quality Time with your Family

The final stage of the Tour de France is a very special time. The hard racing is over. The winners have been decided. All that remains is the ceremonial ride into Paris, culminating with the final laps down the Champs Elysees. There is time to reminisce about the difficult stages, toast the winners with a glass of champagne, and pay respect to those who wear the coveted yellow jersey.

The final stage of your Tour de Profit is much the same. You've put in your best efforts. The results are all but final. It is now time to celebrate your victories and give thanks for all the good things that happened for you throughout the year. There will be time to compete again, but for now, the focus is on celebration and appreciation.

While you road hard throughout the year, and focused on your business, the final measure of success comes down to the satisfaction you have in your personal life. It matters more to have improved your relationship with your spouse or significant other, and your children. You've spent the majority of your time in and around your business; now is the time to focus on your family, your important relationships, and yourself.

Your business often becomes the beacon that guides your life and consumes your time. If you have a healthy balance throughout the year, then good for you! Unfortunately, most do not. If you are among those who run hard and fast all year long, then this stage is designed with you in mind. This is your time to step away from the business and enjoy the fruits of your hard work.

And, don't forget to allow your team members to do the same. Be considerate of what matters to your team members, and give them the flexibility and freedom to refresh and recharge.

I hope you are proud of what you have accomplished during the Tour de Profit. Now is the time to rest up before you have to get back on the bike for next year's ride. The course continues to get more difficult. The route changes each year, and new opportunities await.

Here's wishing you the best as we bring this year's race to a close. We'll be ready to push you along as you gear up for next year. I look forward to riding along with you again as you continue your quest to win the Tour de Profit.

APPENDIX
Frequently Asked Questions for ActionCOACH

1. So, who is ActionCOACH?

ActionCOACH is the world's #1 business coaching firm. Started in 1993 by founder and CEO Brad Sugars, Action-COACH is the fastest growing company of its kind in the world, with offices and Business Coaches from Singapore to Sydney to San Francisco. From the start, ActionCOACH has been set up with you, the business owner, in mind.

As an alternative to conventional and costly consulting firms, ActionCOACH is designed to give you both short-term assistance and long-term training through its afford-able and effective mentoring approaches.

After years of workshops, group coaching sessions, and one-on-one coaching programs focused on our exclusive business building strategies, ActionCOACH has attracted more than 10,000 clients and more than 500,000 seminar attendees who will attest to the power of our programs.

Based on sales, marketing, and business manage-ment systems, ActionCOACH not only shows you how to increase your business revenues and profits (often quite dramatically), but also how to develop your business so that you, as the owner, can work less, relax more, and enjoy business ownership.

Our Business Coaches have substantial business experience, and are fellow business owners who have invested their time, money, and energy to make their own various business ventures successful.

Your success truly does determine our success.

2. Why do I need a Business Coach?

Every great performer, whether an athlete, business owner, or entertainer, is surrounded by coaches or advisors.

As the world of business moves faster and gets more competitive, it's difficult to keep up with all the changes in your industry, in addition to running your business every day.

Just like great athletes find success by following the lead of a coach with a winning game plan, more business owners than ever before are turning to Business Coaches to help develop a winning game plan for their businesses.

Why?

First of all, it's very difficult to be truly objective about yourself. A Business Coach can be objective for you, and can see the "forest for the trees."

A sports coach will make you focus on the game and will make you run more laps than you feel like. A good coach will also tell it like it is, and will give you small pointers about the game and your competition. A great coach will listen and guide you to success.

Likewise, a Business Coach will make you focus on your business, and hold you accountable to the things you should do and to where you want your business to be. A good Business Coach will also be your marketing manager, your sales director, your training coordinator, your partner, your confidant, your mentor, and your best friend.

More importantly, your ActionCOACH will help you make your dreams come true.

3. What's an Alignment Consultation?

Great question. The Alignment Consultation is where an ActionCOACH starts with every business owner.

Your investment includes a two to three hour meeting with your ActionCOACH. During this meeting your ActionCOACH will learn as much as possible about your business, your goals, your challenges, your sales, your marketing, your finances, and so much more.

Everything is done with three goals in mind: First, to know exactly where your business is now. Second, to clarify your business and personal goals. And third, to get the crucial pieces of information needed to create an Action-PLAN for your business over the next 12-months.

The plan isn't a traditional business or marketing plan, but rather a step-by-step plan of action you'll work through as you continue through the duration of our one-on-one coaching program.

4. So, what is one-on-one coaching?

Simply put, it's one of our most popular programs, and it's the only program in which your ActionCOACH will work with you one-on-one for a full 12 months to make all of your goals a reality.

From weekly coaching calls and goal setting sessions, to creating your new marketing pieces, you will develop new sales strategies and business systems so you can work less and learn all you need to know to make your dreams come true.

Your monthly investment ensures your ActionCOACH will dedicate a minimum of five hours a month to work with you on your sales, marketing, team building, business development, and every element of the ActionPLAN you created during your Alignment Consultation.

Unlike a consultant, your personal ActionCOACH will do more than just show you what to do; he or she will be with you when you need them most as each idea takes shape, as each campaign is put into place, as you need the little pointers to make things happen. Your ActionCOACH will also be there when you need someone to talk to, when you're faced with challenges, or most importantly, when you're just not sure what to do next.

Your ActionCOACH will be there every step of the way.

5. Why at least 12 months?

If you've been in business for more than a few weeks, you've seen at least one or two so-called "quick fixes." Most consultants seem to think they can solve all your problems in a few hours or a few days.

At ActionCOACH, we believe long-term success means not just doing it for you; it means doing it with you, showing you how to do it, working alongside you, and creating success together.

Over the course of 12 months, you'll work on different areas of your business.

Each month, you'll not only see your goals become a reality, you'll gain both the confidence and the knowledge to make it happen again and again—even when your first 12 months of coaching is over.

6. How can you be sure this will work in my industry and in my business?

ActionCOACH is expert in the areas of sales, marketing, business development, business management, and team building. With literally hundreds of different profit-building strategies, you'll soon see how truly powerful our systemized approaches are.

Because you are the expert in your business and industry, together we can apply our systems to make your business more effective.

Because of our network of more than 1,000 offices around the world, there is not a business, industry or category our Business Coaches haven't either worked with, managed, worked in, or even owned that is the same or very similar to yours.

Our extensive network means when you hire an ActionCOACH, you hire the full resources of the entire ActionCOACH team to find a solution for any and every challenge you may have. Imagine hiring a company with the collective knowledge of hundreds of experts ready to help you.

7. Won't this just mean more work?

Of course. When you set the plan with your Action-COACH, it may seem a bit overwhelming, but no one ever said attaining your goals would be easy.

In the first few months, it will take some work to adjust to your new plans, but the further you work into the program, the less work you'll actually have to do.

You will, however, be amazed at how focused you'll be and how much you'll get done.

With focus, an ActionCOACH, and most importantly the ActionCOACH systems, you'll be achieving a whole lot more with the same or even less work and effort.

8. How will I find the time?

Again, the first few months will be the toughest, not because of an extra amount of work, but because of how differently you'll work. In fact, your ActionCOACH will show you how, on a day-to-day basis, to get more work done with much less effort.

In other words, after the first few months you'll find that you're not working more, just working differently.

Then, depending on your goals, from about month six onwards, you'll start to see the results of all your work, and if you choose, you can start working less than ever before. Just remember, it's about changing what you do with your time, NOT putting in more time.

9. How much will this cost?

Your investment will depend on the size of your business and the scope of our undertaking together. Your ActionCOACH will work this out with you so it will be appropriate for your business and the goals you want to achieve.

You'll find having an ActionCOACH is just like having a marketing manager, sales team leader, trainer, recruitment specialist, and consultant—all for one nominal investment.

Everything you do with your personal ActionCOACH is a true investment in your future. Not only will you begin to create great results in your business, but you'll end up with an entrepreneurial education that is second-to-none. With that knowledge, you'll be able to repeat your business success over and over again in other ventures.

10. Will it cost me extra to implement the strategies?

Again, give your ActionCOACH just a half-hour and you'll be shown how to turn your marketing into an investment that yields sales and profits rather than just running up your expenses.

We have a system that works. We know how to achieve our goals and can now leave our business and go on lengthy holidays.

In most cases, an ActionCOACH will actually save you money when that coach discovers areas that aren't working for you or your business. For some marketing programs, you will need to spend some money to make some money.

Yet, when you follow our simple testing and measuring systems, you'll never risk more than a few dollars on each campaign.

And when we find the campaigns that work, we make sure you keep profiting from them time and again.

Remember, when you default to the accounting way of saving costs, you can only add a few percentage points to your bottom line.

Following the ActionCOACH formulas, your returns from your sales and marketing can be exponential.

11. Are there any guarantees?

Yes! As the leading coaching company in the world, we are also the only coaching company of any kind to guarantee our work, and that you will get results!

Remember, though we are still your Business Coach, we can't do your work for you. You´re still the player, and it will always be up to you to take the field.

We will push you, cajole you, help you, be there for you, and even do some things with you. But in the end, you've still got to do the work.

Ultimately, only YOU can ever be truly accountable and responsible for your own success.

We will guarantee to provide the best service and support available, to answer your questions and challenges promptly, and offer you the most current and appropriate processes and approaches.

Finally, we are fully committed to helping you become successful (whether you like it at the time or not).

That´s right. Once we've helped you set your goals and create your plan, we'll do whatever it takes to make sure that you achieve your goals, at the same time, promoting a balanced lifestyle as an overriding theme in all we do.

This is to ensure you never compromise either the long-term health and success of your or your company, or your personal values, and what's most important to you.

12. What results have other business owners seen?

Everything from owners previously working 60 hours a week down to working just 10, or revenue increases 100's and even 1,000's of percent. Our results speak for themselves, and are highlighted by specific examples featuring real people with real businesses.

There are three main reasons why this will work for you and your business. First, your ActionCOACH will help you get 100% focused on your goals and the step-by-step processes to get you there. This focus alone is amazing in its effect on you and your business results.

Second, your ActionCOACH will hold you accountable to get things done, not just the day-to-day running of the business, but for the dynamic growth of the business. You're making an investment in your success—and we're going to get you there.

Third, your ActionCOACH is going to teach you as many of our 328 profit building strategies as you may need.

So, whether your goal is to make more money or work less hours or both within the next 12-months, we will work with you to make your goals a reality.

But don't take our word for it; ask any of the thousands of existing ActionCOACH clients, check out the results on our website, or ask your ActionCOACH for a copy of our global testimonial DVD *Action Speaks Louder Than Words*.

13. What areas will you coach me in?

We will work with you in five key areas, and the emphasis in each will depend on you, your business, and of course your goals.

These key areas are:

- Sales: The backbone for creating a profitable business, and one of the areas we'll help you get spectacular results in.

- Marketing and Advertising: If you want to make a sale, you've first got to find a prospect. Over the next 12 months your ActionCOACH will teach you amazingly simple, yet powerful, streetwise marketing techniques, and approaches that will drive profits.

- Team Building and Recruitment: You'll never just wish to find the right people again. You'll have motivated, passionate, enthusiastic, and loyal team members for your business when your Action-COACH shows you how.

- Systems and Business Development: End the hopeless cycle of "the business running you" and begin running your business. We will show you the secrets of having your business "work" even when you're not there.

- Customer Service: Discover how to deliver your product or service consistently, making it easy for your customers to buy and leaving them feeling delighted with your service. Learn new ways to motivate your current customers to give you referrals and to ensure their repeat business. These are just two of the many strategies we will teach you.

14. Can you also train my people?

Yes, in fact, we believe that training your people is almost as important as coaching you.

Your ActionCOACH can provide you and your business with many different training modules, including TeamRICH, SalesRICH, PhoneRICH, and ServiceRICH. You'll be amazed at how much enthusiasm and commitment comes from your team as they experience each of our training programs.

15. Can you write ads, letters and marketing pieces for me?

Yes. Your ActionCOACH can do it for you. Your Action-COACH can also train you to do it yourself, or simply critique the marketing pieces you're using right now.

Should you want us to do it for you, you won't get just one piece. We'll design several for you to take to the market to test which one is the best performer. If it's just a critique you're after, we'll work through your piece and offer feedback in terms of what to change, how to change it, and what else you should do to make it effective. Finally, we can recommend a variety of books or resource materials which provide a "home study" opportunity for you so you'll know how to do it yourself next time.

16. Why do you also recommend books and DVDs?

We do this to save you both time and money. You can learn the basics in your own time so when we get together we'll be working on higher level implementations rather than the basics.

It's also a very powerful way for you to speed up the coaching process and get phenomenal–rather than just great–results.

17. When is the best time to get started?

Right now! Before you take another step, waste another dollar, lose another sale, work too many more hours, miss another family event, or forget another special occasion, you need to call ActionCOACH today.

Far too many business people wait and see, thinking that working harder will make everything better. Remember, what you know got you where you are today. To get where you want to go, you've got to make some changes, and most likely, you'll have to learn something new.

There's no time like the present to get started on your dreams and goals.

18. So, how do we get started?

First, you need to get back in touch with your Action-COACH. There's some very simple paperwork to sign and you're on your way.

Next, you'll need to invest a few hours showing your coach everything about your business.

Together you'll get a plan created, and then the work really starts!

Remember, it may seem like a big job at the start, but with an ActionCOACH, you're sharing the load.

Together, we'll achieve great things!

ABOUT THE AUTHOR

Starting with his father's small family business, Rich has had a storybook career. With experience in both large and small businesses, Rich decided to retire early from the corporate life and focus his efforts on helping business leaders achieve their dreams and significantly grow their business.

A former Captain in the U.S. Army, Rich holds a BS in Accounting from Arizona State University and an MBA in International Business from the University of Texas at Dallas.

Rich worked for Texas Instruments for 14 years, achieving the level of VP, Human Resources. He then joined Pella Corporation as VP HR where he led the effort to get Pella recognized on *Fortune Magazine's* 100 Best Places to Work for seven straight years. While still with Pella, he assumed leadership of their Entry Systems Division as Division President. Rich led the Entry Systems Division for six years during which time the business increased sales by over 400%, improved profitability by over 300% and created new jobs for over 400 people. He retired from Pella in 2005.

Rich joined ActionCOACH, the World's #1 Business Coaching practice, as an Executive & Business Coach in 2007. As a Coach, Rich works one-to-one with business owners, corporate executives and organizational leaders to think through the many challenges and issues that face businesses and organizations today. Rich works with the senior-most leader to create an enterprise that:

- Is built on a solid foundation
- Has a unique position in the marketplace
- Operates on a high-performance Business Chassis
- Is grounded in repeatable processes
- Is operated by a motivated and skilled team of people
- Is lead by a visionary leader

Business leaders who work with Rich learn how to create this powerful business model, and gain the benefits of achieving their dream!

Rich is active in his community and has held positions on several business and non-profit boards including: the Frisco Chamber of Commerce, located in Frisco TX; Prosper Chamber of Commerce, located in Prosper TX; University of Texas at Dallas Executive Education Advisory Board; ActionCOACH Coaching for a Cause Campaign; ManeGait Therapeutic Horsemanship, based in McKinney TX; Genesis Elevator Company, based in Atlanta, GA; and Unity Resources, based in Plano TX.

Rich has been named Coach of the Year in North Texas for 2007 and 2008, was recognized as BrandCOACH for the Americas in 2009, and was recognized as the 2009 Entrepreneur of the Year by the Frisco Chamber of Commerce.

Rich and his wife, Drew, live in Prosper, Texas, with their three children: Megan, Rhett, and Anne Drew.

Rich has a passion for sports, particularly running. He has completed the Boston Marathon.

Rich recognizes that "Successful business leaders know how to surround themselves with a strong team of advisors who can help them think through the most difficult business challenges." Rich is energized by helping business leaders realize their dreams and achieve what they believe is impossible.